Monday - talk w/ liz
12:30 call
Andrea- 818 707 6969

A Triumph of Love

By

Andrea Berman Matis

~ Serenaid ~

The Matis Family At The Pool

Original Acrylic Painting by Andrea Berman Matis

~ Serenaid ~

~ Serenaid ~

Williams Publishing Company
6176 Driver Road
Palm Springs, CA 92264

Library of Congress Control Number: LCCN 2007935551
ISBN: 978-0-9666906-6-8

Cover Art by Kareen Ross
All other art and design by Arte Moderno and Wild Beast Productions

Publisher's Cataloging-In-Publication Data
(Prepared by The Donohue Group, Inc.)

Matis, Andrea Berman.
  Serenaid : a triumph of love / by Andrea Berman Matis.

    p. : ill. ; cm.

  ISBN: 978-0-9666906-6-8

1. Matis, Andrea Berman. 2. Adoptive parents--Biography.
3. Scleroderma (Disease)--Patients--Biography. I. Title.

HV874.82.M38 A3 2007
362.7/34/092   2007935551

Printed in The United States of America
10 9 8 7 6 5 4 3 2

~ Serenaid ~

Be who you are and say what you feel,
because those who mind don't matter
and those who matter, don't mind.

Dr. Seuss

~ Serenaid ~

About The Author

Andrea Berman Matis

Andrea Berman Matis is an accomplished dancer, loving wife and mother of three. She has a Master of Arts Degree in Dance and Movement Therapy and a Certificate of Dance from the Laban Centre for Dance at the University of London. She has been a professional dancer, mime, teacher, and choreographer for the past 30 years. Her diagnosis of Scleroderma in 1983 has been an obstacle, but it didn't stop her from founding the Universal Scleroderma Foundation and working with the Arthritis Foundation of Southern California and the Scleroderma Research Foundation. Andrea lives with her husband and children in Oak Park, California.

~ Serenaid ~

~ Serenaid ~

Acknowledgements

Thanks to all of the wonderful people who encouraged me and helped me to write this story.

Katherine and Mark Kelley, Jean and Norman Berman, Scott Matis, Bruce Seren Matis, Blaine Esty Matis, Brooke Ronit Matis, Miriam Berman, Bill Rose, Ph.D., Chelsea and Torrey Kelley, Kerry Rose, Marjorie Rose, Kathleen Foley, Jeffrey Galpin, M.D., Lillian Szydlo, M.D., Bob Saget, Jackie Zabel, Morgan Most, Quincie Melville, Ziona Friedlander, Cathy Russoff O'Neill, Fern Galperin, Benita Roth, Rosalind Gottfried, Paula Roberts, Anne Cohen, Leslie Williams, Joyce Gregg, Laura Pope, Clyde Phillips, James Egan, Nancy Greenberg Concool, Kim Kuciel, Janis Zloto and Cinder Bond.

Dedicated to the Memory of Aunt Gale Matis.

This entire book was originally composed and typed with just two fingers.

~ Serenaid ~

Contents

~ Serenaid ~

Chapter One

And Now We Were Ready

On November 29th, 1981, I married Scott, my on-again, off-again boyfriend of eight years. We were both twenty-seven, with good jobs and hopeful futures. As Scott would say, the world was our oyster. Scott owned a restaurant called 'The Wiener Factory' in Sherman Oaks, California and I was working for an accomplished literary agent in Beverly Hills. We were the ultimate DINK's, double income, no kids. But that was about to change. Marriage was the huge plunge that would soon make us a family, the family we always talked about that we would someday have when we were ready. And now we were ready.

We received two very different responses when we told our respective parents of the upcoming nuptials. Scott's mom, Millie asked me, "Are you pregnant?" My mom, Jean asked Scott, "Have you had long enough to think about it? Was eight years sufficient?" Together, as best friends, we were to have a marriage made in heaven.

Scott and I met on February 4th, 1973 in Clyde Phillip's Freshman English 101 class at California State University, Northridge. I had met Clyde running for classes in the English Department hallway the week before and begged him to let me into his class, since I could not get the required English 101 class my first semester. He told me he would do the best he could, and for me to show up that first Tuesday morning at 7:45. He asked for my name so he would remember me and I told him, "Andrea Berman." He said, "I used to date a girl named Andrea Berman at UCLA". My response to that was, "Yeah, sure you did..." assuming it was some type of pick up line, as I was always the skeptic. Clyde was a 23-year-old UCLA graduate student at the time, but he did remember me and signed me in his class the following week. At the same time, he also added a young man named Scott, who was wearing beige desert boots with no socks and a plaid flannel shirt with Levi jeans. Quite an 'east coast' style of clothing, I thought for conservative southern California at that time. He looked like he was from Philly or New York. Of course, I was in my embroidered peasant dress and faux shearling lined suede boots, having recently moved to the San Fernando Valley from New Jersey. So who's to judge? To those that didn't know me, I was the girl who went to Jewish socialist sleep away camp, like the stereotypical Allison in the Woody Allen movie "Annie Hall".

As time went by, I became quite friendly with Scott. We got together over a bag of marshmallows. The marshmallow story goes like this: we were reading *The Lottery* by Shirley Jackson, in Freshman English. If you don't know, it's the story about crowds stoning people to death. Clyde had the class act it out. He divided us into two groups. One group stood together at the front of the room and the other stood in the back and we tossed multi colored marshmallows across the room at each other. Then, one by one, Clyde took one person away from each group and had the 'stoning' continue, until it was just down to two people. The power and strength of the group had dissipated and Scott and I, as the last two participants, were on our own to attack. I was the thrower, Scott the target. Not to be influenced by the crowd mentality, I continued to pummel Scott with marshmallows. Clyde, obviously a clairvoyant, knew something about relationships, leaving the two of us until the end. Indeed he indeed did know something about writing and about people, as he went on to become a successful TV show creator and producer as well as a novelist and one of the inspirations to write this story! Fast forward eight years.

Our Thanksgiving weekend wedding was the best Jewish wedding I had ever been to, and my family and friends all agree. My parents spared no expense, from the roses to the gown and the Jeff Caron Band singing Springsteen's Hungry Heart; it was all done to the hilt. I remember the search for the wedding gown. I started at the Gibson Girl on Ventura Boulevard in Tarzana. My favorite dress there was pure white, off the shoulder with a pearled fitted bodice and full length skirt. It was very low cut and I would have had to wear a shawl of some sort for the ceremony in the synagogue, which I could later remove for the reception. I decided to completely investigate Bridal Shops all over the San Fernando Valley, the Westside and Beverly Hills. I fell in love with another dress in Los Angeles, but to be perfectly sure, headed back one more time to the Gibson Girl to double check my original dress. While in the dressing room, the saleswoman came in and said they had one new dress I might like to see before making the big decision. She brought me a very traditional off white, high collared pearl beaded lace trimmed gown. On the hanger, I thought, 'It's OK", so I put it on. Then, I started to cry and I said to my Mom, "This is the dress." I looked at the price tag and asked if she thought Daddy would pay for it. It was the most expensive piece of clothing I had ever seen. My mother asked if she could borrow the phone, clarifying to the saleswoman that it was of course for a local call. Soon my dad arrived at the store. That was it. He looked at it and it was mine!

Having been a starving dancer and working as a waitress for a caterer to help support myself, I knew all the good florists, photographers and bands to choose for the perfect affair. Relatives from eleven states were there to celebrate with us. We had a nice traditional Jewish Ceremony, because as they say, "No, Chuppa, no Schtuppa!" We were then driven to the Universal Sheraton for our reception in a classic white Bentley. We greeted our 247 guests, dined, danced and celebrated wholeheartedly. We honeymooned the following morning starting with the flight to New York. My honeymoon wardrobe was packed and consisted of a variety of very cute clothes, from plaid laced knickers to a camouflage mini dress, all of which were not warm enough to sustain me in the freezing London, Paris and Swiss climates. I bought a pair of brown suede boots in Marks and Spencer (or Marks and Sparks as the British girls taught me to say) to go along with the leopard pants I found while shopping in London on Oxford Street.

The sun was barely up when we boarded the bus from the Sheraton Universal to LAX. We were barely up ourselves. The first leg of the trip was to Kennedy Airport in New York. I recalled being there ten years earlier for my first ever airplane flight. I was seventeen and had written an essay and won a scholarship to travel to Israel for the entire summer, sightseeing and living on a kibbutz, a collective farm in the Galilee section of Israel. I didn't know one person when my parents left me in the terminal to wait out an eight-hour electrical storm. I met lots of other teens and had an enlightening summer. I was fascinated by Jerusalem and the Sea of Galilee. I learned about other religions and the people of the Middle East.

However, this time, I was with my husband on a layover to London Heathrow for my honeymoon! We picked up a newspaper while waiting for the flight segment to London to pass the time and were shocked to see the headline that Natalie Wood had drowned. My whole life I had been told that I looked like her by all of my parents friends, especially as a child after *Miracle on 34th Street*, and so she always held a very special place in my heart. I had seen all of her movies and read all about her. I was so upset to hear the news. One of my dance teachers even called me Natalie for years. My mom later told me that she knew all about it at my wedding, but also knew it would upset me and so she had decided not to tell me.

We arrived in London the next morning in a daze. Scott and I found a black cab and hopped right in. I felt at home as I had lived there in the late seventies while getting a post graduate Certificate of Dance from the Laban Centre for Dance at the University of London.

My love for dance began when I was five years old. Every Saturday morning, I would wake up and walk up the block from my house to Susan Wise's house further up 40th Street in Wilmington, Delaware. I was joined by my cousin Sheri and the other neighborhood usual suspects. From ten to eleven o'clock, we would pay our dime and have our dance lesson in Susan's basement. Twenty minutes of ballet (I was very limber), twenty minutes of tap (I had great rhythm) and twenty minutes of acrobats (I was a tumbling fool). Big mirrors leaned against the cinder block walls as we watched ourselves dance and practice for recitals where we performed such numbers as, "Daisy, Daisy" and "Twinkle, Twinkle." Afterwards we went upstairs to her mother Helen's kitchen and had our milk and Oreo cookies. I did this for three years, until I started Sunday school and went to Sabbath services on my Saturday mornings thereafter.

By the time I was in sixth grade, the dancing bug returned and I asked my mother if I could please take ballet lessons. All by myself, I would take the bus from 40th Street to 14th Street to the Academy of Dance where I would put on my black leotard and pink tights and study ballet under the famous Madame Antonova as she banged her cane on the wooden floors. James Jamieson, the Scottish sword dancer would make his rare appearance from the loft above and correct our feet and hips. By seventh grade, all I wanted to be was a cheerleader and I was the only eighth grader to make the squad and also to make a club called the Leader Corps, the gymnastics and tumbling team at my junior high at that time.

In ninth grade my family and I moved out from our tiny row house in Wilmington to our big brick Normandy Manor home in Teaneck, New Jersey. Although my father, as PTA President and a representative of his community, had refused to leave our high school neighborhood in Delaware after the riots following the assassination of Martin Luther King Jr., his job relocated him to New York City and I began a new school in September, 1968. Soon I was back in ballet class and even started Pointe work. During a performance in a small theater in New Jersey, I was privileged to watch another dancer, Dian Dong, and soon I was taking Modern Dance classes at the Center for the Foundation of Modern Dance (CFMD) in Hackensack. Later, I saw Dian perform with the Kathryn Posin Dance Company from New York, at the University of California, Santa Barbara, where I re-introduced myself after many years. I continued Ballet and Modern dance classes throughout high school and when once again my father was relocated for his job, I continued dancing in sunny southern California.

I started California State University at Northridge (CSUN) in the fall of 1972, (I had actually applied to Valley State College, but was accepted to CSUN when the name changed) where I created my own dance major for the following two years. I performed in many dance and drama productions in the Performing Arts Department at Northridge. I took private lessons from Sheila Rozann in Chatsworth in my spare time (Balanchine technique) when I wasn't working as a choreographer for a children's theatre group at the local Jewish Community Center, and as hard as it was for me, performed with the advanced students (all way younger than I) at their Spring Recital. I was nineteen, they were all in junior high and high school, but adult classes were not of the same caliber and so I took the kids classes. The girls in my ballet class were shocked to see that I could drive! From CSUN, I transferred to the University of California, Santa Barbara (UCSB). I double majored in Dance and Developmental Psychology and again, loved the performing aspects of the dance department. People often told me I reminded them of the dancer, Twyla Tharp. My sense of humor, technique style, performance dynamics and our Dorothy Hamill haircuts were all so similar. Scott would sit in the wings of the campus theatre or on the floor of the dance studio and watch me dance, as he transferred to UCSB after I did. I volunteered to work for a dance therapist in town, where I worked with disabled children and adults and my interests expanded. Joan Smallwood was the President of the American Dance Therapy Association and a mentor for my future. She led the movement groups and guided my course selections. I also loved the dance analysis classes where we studied Labanotation (the writing of dance) and choreography at UCSB.

In the fall of 1976, I was admitted to graduate school at Immaculate Heart College in Hollywood. I continued my studies in analysis, dance therapy, verbal therapeutic techniques and dance technique. In my second year at IHC, when I was working on my Master's Thesis in Dance-Movement Therapy, I read in detail about a woman named Dr. Marion North. She had written a book called *Personality Assessment Through Movement,* and that was it for me. I found myself writing to her and asking her if I could study at her Dance Centre in London. My mother and I flew to San Francisco to interview with a woman named Bonnie Bird who was originally from the Martha Graham Dance Company and head of the Dance and Theatre Division of the Laban Centre for Dance. I was admitted for the following season and as I wrapped up my Masters Degree, I was packing my leotards and tights and heading to London for my Post Graduate Certificate in Dance. It was one of the best years of my life!

Three weeks after I returned from my dance studies in London, I auditioned for and got into Momentum Dance Company in downtown Los Angeles. My professional dance career continued with performing at the John Anson Ford Theatre in Hollywood with the Richard Oliver Dance Company. One of the performances stands out in particular. The Los Angeles Area Dance Alliance Dance Kaleidoscope was the biggest dance performance show in Los Angeles and it was held at a lovely outdoor venue, the John Anson Ford Theater. The day of the show, I went to the beach and got a quickie tan. I dressed in my golden bra and headdress and thought I looked fantastic as I entered from the wings. I shook my spray painted branches and contracted well enough to make even Martha Graham proud. The audience applauded and my modern dance teacher, Charles Edmondson told me I had never danced better. Back stage after the show, my fiancé, Scott, told me he overheard a conversation between his brother Alan and my dad after my performance. Alan turned to my dad and asked, "Norm, what was that about?" And my dad, in all his wit and wisdom replied, "About ten minutes too long."

Later I taught for and performed with the Richmond Shepard Mime Troupe, thinking that someday I would be the next Shields and Yarnell. At last, after many small companies and performances, I found Sarah Elgart, the choreographer of my dreams. I was ecstatic to be working with her and knew I had found my place in the Los Angeles dance scene. I had even told my parents they didn't need to come to my first performance with the Sarah Elgart Company because there would be many more times to see me dance. After my dad's comments about my prior performance, I knew watching contemporary dance was hard for him. Music like the Pretenders may have made it even worse, and I excused him from my next show. I guess this was when I learned that making life plans doesn't always work. My parents had missed my last professional dance performance.

So, back to the honeymoon, there I was, returning to my favorite city on earth with my new husband. I couldn't wait to get to our hotel, the Savoy. I had always wanted to stay there ever since I was a starving dancer exploring all that London had to offer and now Scott had actually booked it for our honeymoon night. The cockney cabbie was so impressed, "So, how much does it cost to stay at the Savoy these days?" he asked. Scott said, "About seventy pounds," and the cabbie broke out in a thunderous laugh, "What Savoy are you staying at?" Scott quickly pulled out our travel papers only to see that the travel agent had booked us at the Savoy Court Hotel on Oxford and Bond Streets. Our disappointment was curbed when we arrived at this gorgeous, quaint hotel and were invited to tea before our room was ready. After settling in, we rested for a few minutes and headed out on "an explore", as Winnie the Pooh would say, by foot. We headed straight to Leicester Square and purchased tickets for that evening's performance of "Amadeus".

The honeymoon was off to a wonderful start and eighteen days of awe and wonder had begun. We couldn't even spend all the money that Scott had brought! After our stay at the Savoy Court, we also stayed for a few days with my dear dancer friend, Katy, from the University of London. It was so cold in Katy and her new husband Tim's flat, that when we woke up, there was actually frost on the walls of our guest bedroom. We traveled and toured all around London. Then we were off to Switzerland for a 'White Week' as they called it: skiing, eating our favorite meal ever at Cherries in Davos, dancing on the oldest bridge in Lucerne and then to Paris to see the Eiffel Tower. We headed back to the States, and back to our jobs before New Year's Eve.

Our married life together began in a two bedroom triplex in Sherman Oaks, walking distance from the Wiener Factory and Ventura Boulevard. We had a new thing, cable TV and our own laundry room and garage. I commuted through Beverly Glen to Breakdown Services in Los Angeles. Breakdown was a casting service offered to the entertainment industry where one could learn all the ins and outs of show biz. In mid January, I contracted one of the worst cases of bronchitis I had ever had. I missed another eight days of work, and was feeling guilt ridden after having just returned from my extended honeymoon vacation. I was on the antibiotic Erythromycin and had a lingering cough beyond Valentine's Day, when we had our very first of many Matis theme parties. Scott returned from the Laker - Boston game just in the nick of time. I wore this great black, skin tight, silk dress I had bought at a jumble sale (what we refer to as a garage sale) while living in London. It was low cut and I looked fabulous. Over the years, we continued our party themes with Valentine's Day, Fancy Dress, Black and White, St. Patrick's Day, Vernal Equinox, Halloween, Mardi Gras, Roaring Twenties, Sixties and the all famous, Toga, Toga, Toga party! As the years passed, our 'Senior Prom' party was a huge hit.

During a slow physical recovery from a hacking cough, house shopping became our next priority. After some searching from Venice Beach all the way to the west valley, we found a tiny little two-bedroom house 'south of the boulevard' in Woodland Hills. Nine hundred square feet of affordable private space on a quarter acre of California land all our own. The backyard was so large that while we meandered through the Topanga Mall one evening, we decided to take home a $20 mutt from Critterville, who we named, Gladys Matis. And so, our family life was beginning.

Shortly after settling into our new home, and my cough finally subsiding, I began to have some additional strange new physical symptoms. I thought, maybe I'm allergic to Gladys, or maybe the rose bushes or mint in the front of the house were causing my fingers and hands to swell. But when my hands turned navy blue at work one day, the same color as my favorite jumpsuit, I knew something was terribly wrong. "Peter," I said to the vice president at work, "What do you think of this?" I showed him my purple fingers and his face went white. "I think you need to see a doctor immediately."

The next day I was off to my old internist who in turn, sent me to my new rheumatologist. Dr. Peng Fan started calling me 'the kid' whenever I arrived, as most of his clientele was well over 50 and here I was, having just recently turned twenty-eight. It didn't take long for him to tell me that I had what was called Raynaud's phenomenon, a vascular circulatory illness that was like frostbite. I headed back to work on vaso-dilators to keep my blood flowing to my extremities. By June, my condition had worsened and I started to develop painful ulcerations on my fingertips and was told I needed to go on disability for a while and not work. Dr. Fan had been hoping it was only Raynaud's, but deep down, as I watched him examine my fingernail beds under a microscope, I knew he thought otherwise.

The conflicts started to arise. I had just changed jobs at work from Breakdown Services to Writers and Artists Agency in Beverly Hills, a job I had interviewed for several times. For my third interview to be a Literary Agent Assistant, I was called to come in while I was at work at Breakdown. I had to go to meet with Dan at Writers and Artists Agency again, but I was not dressed for an interview this time. Instead of my usual camel a-lined skirt and burgundy silk blouse with matching pumps, I had on my white poplin button down collared shirt, with a black and white with silver highlights 50's flared skirt and my white jazz dance shoes for walking the studio lots. I even had on bobby sox. And I got the job! I was ecstatic, looking towards my future being an agent, a producer, a casting director, who knows? It was difficult leaving my job at Breakdown. I had learned so much about the entertainment industry and loved driving to the studios and talking to casting directors and producers of television and film. I was surrounded by wonderfully creative people. The voyeur in me would erupt when I would see TV and film stars on the MGM lot, or eat in the commissary on the Fox lot. I would keep notes of the famous people I sited so that I would remember later.

I have a favorite story to tell about walking on the back lot at MGM. Back then, my vintage style of clothing was all my own. Even for those days. I was wearing a red French cotton dress with black velvet trim and black Italian leather spike healed ankle boots. It was fun to dress everyday and then walk around the studios as if I was somebody important, not just a glorified messenger from Breakdown. I was walking by the studio store when I heard someone singing to me from behind. "Hey there Little Red Riding Hood." I turn around slowly and there in my face was Eric Estrada singing to me, "You sure are looking good," the old 60's song. My face now matched my dress and I continued walking as fast as I could to my car. Just another day in the life.

At Writers and Artists Agency, my new boss, Dan, and I got along tremendously. Three weeks later, Doctor Fan restricted me to R&R, rest and relaxation for three months. As I maintained a relatively healthy status with no further progression at that time, Dr. Fan let me return to work part-time, but Dan had just finally replaced my assistant position, having waited as long as he could with a temp. I went back to work as an assistant to a talent agent instead, for three days a week. Six weeks later, my next new boss, Tim, left to go out on his own. It was a good thing I had already met his main client, Rob Lowe, beforehand, as now I always have a good story to tell about having met Rob in Tim's office. It wasn't until years later, however, that I actually saw the infamous video Lowe made with a friend and an under aged girl in a hotel room. My girlfriend Joyce had brought the secret video over to my house one day when I wasn't feeling up to par and we watched from my living room sofa. Several years later at Joyce's 40th birthday bash, all the guests were asked to stand and tell a favorite story about Joyce. It was then that I thanked her for allowing me to watch one of the most infamous films made in Hollywood!

After Tim left the agency, I was placed on unemployment and things seemed to work out just fine. Later, I did a couple of 'extra work' jobs in teenage movies, for cash. I even did an episode on "Square Pegs", a TV show with Sarah Jessica Parker, playing a high school kid when I was twenty-eight years old. I loved getting those teenage parts. I was in a movie called "Private School" with Mathew Modine and Phoebe Cates and even did a Miller beer commercial. Nonetheless, the Hollywood excitement was short lived.

In December of 1982, I started getting pains in my chest. We were on a cruise with Scott's family and I was in pain and miserable. I was missing out on all the fun of the Mexican Riviera. I never even made it up to the onboard casino. After the holidays and the New Year rolled around, I was back at Dr. Fan's office. He sent me to another doctor to get a chest X-ray. It appeared that I had fluid in my lungs, but when the doctor tried to extract the liquid, with the biggest needle I had ever seen in my entire life, nothing came out. I was terribly frightened and the test was very painful. A new symptom was starting, scar tissue in my lungs. I was sent home with some Valium to ease the pain and my anxiety. I followed that with a visit to St. Joseph's hospital in Burbank for extensive lung testing. This was the Hospital where Scott was born and he hadn't been back in all those years. After the battery of tests was completed: treadmill, blood gas and various other breathing monitors, it was confirmed that I had lung involvement in whatever was going on in my body. I was the proud owner of lungs with decreased diffusion. There was no remedy.

In the late spring of 1983, it was time for a vacation. My chest still hurt and I had been depressed for quite a while. Then, my cousin Sheri, the doctor, called from Baltimore. Sheri was the big sister I never had.

We grew up taking dance classes together, cheering together, played kickball together and stuck together throughout our lives through thick and thin. She was personality personified. You know when you meet someone and they remind you of someone else? They look or sound or act like someone you already know? Well, in my lifetime, I have NEVER met anyone who reminded me of Sheri. No one could replace her. She is one of a kind, for sure. Sheri and her husband were going to the Caribbean and wanted us to join them. Well, I thought, what could be more uplifting than that? She is one of the most fun people I knew. We grew up across the back alleyway together until I was fourteen and she was fifteen. We could see each other through our kitchen windows and practice our cheerleading movements together. We were best friends, although she was definitely the more boisterous one! As my grandmother, MomMom, always used to say to me, "You should learn by Sheri's mistakes!"

And I did; I learned to be quiet when I needed to and never to 'tattle' on my cousin! MomMom never had to say to me what she said to Sheri on a regular basis, "If you'd listened to me, you wouldn't have to listen to me!"

One day, MomMom decided to 'cure' me. She believed that being from the 'old country', Russia, that she had special spiritual powers. She said she had inherited them from her mother, the town clairvoyant, that she was a 'healer'. She began her ritual by taking an egg out of the refrigerator. She took me into the hallway and began rubbing the egg all over my body from head to toe. Then she marched me into the kitchen where she had a glass bowl half way filled with water. She took the egg and cracked it into the bowl. As the egg hit the water, it began to separate, the white from the yellow. She told me this was the illness in my body separating from me. That it was now going to be gone. It was my first and only "oochsprechen." Maybe she had something there? My mother walked in on us and said to her mother, "Mom, what are you doing? Oochsprechening her?" My MomMom said, "So, what's it to you!" This was a healing spell that MomMom brought with her from Russia. When we used to ask her if she ever wanted to go back to Russia to visit, MomMom who was petrified of flying would always respond, "When they build a bridge."

So, as Sheri directed us, we purchased a Polaroid camera. At the time, there was a special and the camera included a two for one ticket anywhere Delta Airlines flew and we were off to St. Thomas and St. John. What a bargain! It was like heaven on earth. I had never seen such beautiful water or sand in my life. The temperature of the cerulean blue ocean of Trunk Bay was in the 80's and we went to a new beach every day. I didn't realize until my next doctor visit that my beautiful golden brown tan was due to an excess of melanin in my body. Once again, while dining in our rustic wood cabin on St. John Island, a new symptom arose, one I was not familiar with yet. My esophagus decided not to work properly, a sandwich got caught on its way down and I couldn't breathe. I panicked and ran to Sheri in the next room. She quickly got me a glass of water and made me painfully drink it all. As my temporary doctor, she told me to make sure I had an upper G.I. when I returned home.

It was also on this trip where we spent a day sailing that was one of the most wonderful highlights of my life. We sailed to the deserted Caribbean Island, Sandy Key, on the most beautiful sunny day. I had on my perfect island dress, turquoise muslin with a matching sash for a headband. We lunched, played Frisbee on the beach, well, at least the others played Frisbee as I watched, and we all saw dolphins as they chased us by the side of the boat, a sign of good luck.   I would mentally return to this day many times in the future, as an active visualization, when I needed to relax. If I needed to get an I.V. stick, a biopsy or simply to rid my mind of any pain, Sandy Key was my own personal mantra.

The new gastrointestinal tests showed that the lower two thirds of my esophagus had decreased motility, and not only was it difficult for food to go down, but it was also very difficult for anything that went down, to stay down. The confirmed diagnosis was a disease I had never heard of, Scleroderma. Progressive Systemic Sclerosis is a connective tissue disease caused by the overproduction of collagen. It can attack your body wherever it wants, as tissue is everywhere, and its severity varies with each patient. "Life threatening" was not a phrase I wanted to hear, or autoimmune, disability, or infertility. The future looked very dark. I wasn't even thirty yet.

Active visualization and the visions of the Caribbean would come in handy over the next few years and would be used during Biofeedback, Acupuncture and other therapies. Several visits to different psychic healers scared the crap out of me, but alas, none were spot on. Ulcerations on my fingers continued to develop and worsen. The many meds I had been on from Dr. Fan were not doing anything to help and were hard on my stomach, which lead to taking other meds. I was soon referred to an experimental drug study at the UCLA hospital to be a guinea pig, for one Dr. Phillip Clements. I left the warmth and comfort of my own bed, which had the head raised on cinder blocks for my digestion, and headed to Westwood.

I was admitted overnight for baseline testing, my first sleepover ever at a hospital. Blue and white print hospital gowns became my new clothing staple over the next few years: green and white would become a highlight, just as pull-on leggings from Nordstrom and anything Velcro from sneakers to the 501 Levi's that my sister would make wearable for me by removing the buttons and sewing Velcro in their place. They monitored my heart. I had more testing for my lungs, along with blood and urine tests, and they placed me in a double blind study that required me to go off all other medications. No one knew, including me or the doctors, if I had gotten the experimental drug, Ketanserin, or a placebo, a sugar pill used in experimental research. I progressively became sicker and sicker with terrible infections on my fingers, hands, wrists and arms. My girlfriend, Margie, would drive me to Westwood on a regular basis for follow-ups. Being a Grateful Dead fan, I referred to her as very 'Deadicated' to helping me in this strange new time. As they put my hands in freezing water, then re-heated them with a blow-dryer (truly state of the art experiment), Margie waited in the hall to drive me home with great patience. Occasionally I would see hallucinogenic-type light trails from the experimental drug and experienced other odd feelings. We were slowly all becoming aware of the phrase, "expect the worse and hope for the best."

It was then that Sheri's older brother, Robert, the other doctor in the family, became concerned about my health status, as well. He sent me on a holistic doctor hunt to find a man from Germany who was in Phoenix, Arizona at the time. Dr. Voll met with me and in turn, referred me to another doctor in Las Vegas. So I was off to meet Dr. Robert Milne at the Las Vegas Clinic of Preventative Medicine. My mom accompanied me on a trip into a new world of alternative type muscle testing, DMSO (a new medicinal pain treatment for me), vitamins, homeopathy, and nutrition. When I got back home, I was still so full of infected ulcerations that I was soon admitted to UCLA Hospital to receive intravenous antibiotics to help rid me of the osteomyolitis in the bones in my hands and fingers.

I was there for over two weeks of the Christmas holiday season under the admitting care of my new doctor from the study, Dr. Clement's associate, Dr. Lillian Szydlo. The first night there, the hospital was so over-crowded; I was placed on the cancer ward with three other roommates, but it seemed like they were inmates to me. They were moaning and groaning all night and truly freakin' me out! It took eight hours to get the IV antibiotics ordered and delivered. Scott's good friend, Richard Kacik came to relieve Scott so that he could get some rest and go to work in the morning. He held my hand through the next few hours, and to this day has never let go. Dr. Szydlo had me paged to come to the nurse's station, so that she could tell me on the phone that I would not lose any of my fingers and that everything was going to be Okay (the good old EGBOK theory). When the meds were finally administered and starting to take effect and I was more relaxed and in less pain, Richard left me for a good night's sleep. The next day I was under the care of the many curious residents and interns, being asked gazillions of questions and prodded for hours from here to there. At last, I was moved to a semi private room, with roommate Gloria Swanson (no kidding, that was her real name.) My guests greeted her and her guests greeted me for the holidays. It was overall a horrific experience for me from the moment I got there, to the moment I came home with full-time nursing care around the clock, including New Year's Eve. The only highlight was the dinner Scott brought in for me at UCLA from our favorite restaurant, Albion's Bistro, in Studio City on all of our new Royal Albert wedding china and silver. The hall nurses watched while we ate our wild mushroom (from Santa Barbara) soup and glazed duck in peppercorn sauce, shrimp in fifteen spices, and apple tort, while the IV antibiotic line ran through me. I felt more like a Princess than a patient. We were attempting to celebrate the two of us, no matter what the setting. After arriving home, the nurses stayed for another three weeks of vein poking. Then I ran out of good veins and went back to just taking my Ketanserin orally.

Although I continued to remain on the drug study at UCLA, I became sicker and sicker. My state of health and emotions were poor and we decided to take a vacation back to the Caribbean with the couple we had met at Carla's Cottages with Cousin Sheri on St. John the year before. I tried my best to enjoy the beautiful island and amazing French food in St. Bart's, but had so many ulcerations on my hands and arms that I returned to UCLA as soon as we got back to the states. After spending Christmas in the hospital, I returned at Easter to a private room, because I had another staff infection. Scott and I had already founded the Universal Scleroderma Foundation by this time with friends and family volunteering to help us educate patients and raise funds for scleroderma research. Our first fundraiser, a garage sale at the home of our dear friends, Dr. Robert Gold and Kerry Rose, raised over two thousand dollars, but I couldn't be there to share in the excitement, because I was still in the hospital. This was a huge accomplishment for all of us newcomers in non-profit work and we were elated. We were later to hold many more fundraisers including a huge dinner at the Universal Hilton where we honored Dr. Szylo. Keith Carradine was our honorary host and Fritz Coleman, our local NBC weatherman and comedian, entertained us with his comedy. Years later, we folded our group and donated our funds to the Arthritis Foundation and the Scleroderma Research Foundation.

Meanwhile I was spending my days residing at UCLA once again. I was receiving intravenous antibiotics and painful biopsies of the ulcerations on my fingers caused by staff infections. On the other hand, Scott was busy trying to open the second Wiener Factory in Woodland Hills with his new partner, Leslie Uggams, the actress who played "Miss Kizzy" in the mini series, "Roots", and her husband Graham Pratt. They were regular customers in Sherman Oaks and came to Scott and his partner, Kevin, to open another restaurant. We were ready to embark on a new venture of a chain of Weiner Factories and hoping for success with the second shop. This venture, however, was somewhat short-lived.

In late 1983, the movie, "Terms of Endearment" came out. From the trailers on TV, everyone seemed to think it was a comedy with Jack Nicholson and Shirley McClain. So, after our anniversary Thanksgiving dinner with my family, we decided on a family movie. Little did we know that it contained segments about cancer that were devastatingly depressing and emotionally draining. There is a scene in it where the mother, Aurora, (Shirley McClain) throws a tantrum when her daughter is in need of pain medication. Well, my Mom used that scene at UCLA when I was so miserable and the hand specialist had not been to see me after orders had been written. My mom, Jean, asked the nurse if she had ever seen "Terms of Endearment" and said that if the hand surgeon was not on his way any minute, that the scene from the movie would be nothing compared to what she was going to do. I was amazed and impressed by her courage to fight; I had rarely seen her in that form. The doctor was there that afternoon! It was excruciating for my mom to watch her own daughter become so ill. She tried to be calm in front of her family and friends, but sometimes her anxiety was hard to conceal.

Chapter Two

Pathways to Parenthood

By June of 1984, I was beginning to feel better. We had been to counseling therapy, both together and separately, and I was dealing with my day to day functioning, activities of daily living (ADL-as I later taught for the Arthritis Foundation Workshop), and coming to grips with my new life. Velcro and elastic waistbands replaced all shoelaces and zippers. I decided to plan a surprise 30th birthday party for Scott. Our friend, Robert Kacik, Richard's brother, volunteered his new home in Agoura Hills and I invited everyone out to the real 'burbs' to celebrate. I made my first photo collage of the 'Life and Times of Scott Matis' and the party was a huge success. I felt great doing something constructive and being with so many of my friends and family for the day. It was on this very day that my doctor friend and confidant from the UCLA study, Lilly, (Dr. Szydlo) and I were seriously talking honestly about the possible progression of my illness and about starting the family that Scott and I so desperately wanted after all of these years. She told me that Scleroderma generally has a five year progression before signs of stability emerge. Being at the three year plus mark, Lilly could not guarantee that my feeling better at that time was a permanent sign and suggested we begin researching alternatives to starting a family, especially adoption. The possibility of kidney involvement and other problems was too real to try to get pregnant just yet. The chances of getting kidney involvement after the first five years were much less. I started my research with great enthusiasm. There was much to learn.

I soon found out that I could adopt a baby from Mexico in two weeks from an attorney. But, I wasn't ready just yet. I wanted to learn all about adoption, attorneys, state and private agencies. At that time the law in California stated that if you adopted through an attorney, the birth mother had a six month rescission period. In other words, you could adopt a baby and the birthmother had six months in which she could change her mind and decide to take her baby back. If you adopted through a private agency, this period was only two weeks, and then the agency would become the legal guardian if there were any problems. At this point, I chose the latter with the three years of illness I had already been through, I didn't want to be that small percentage of adoptive families whose birth mother may change her mind months later. I had already been through enough. Having an adopted baby taken back by its birth mother would have been devastating.

Scott and I, both together and separately, continued therapy to deal with the many issues that come along with chronic illness. We received comments like, how many meds are you on, when are you going back to work, and when are you going to get pregnant, which all had to go in one ear and out the other. There was no room for negative vibes in our lives. We moved on to the introductory courses at the adoption agency, applications, more counseling, home studies and letters of reference. This was a two year process during which I continued to have medical problems. I continued to detox, went back to the hospital for more I.V. antibiotics and practiced R&R, rest and reflux (acid reflux)! The Los Angeles Olympics came and went and we saw swimmers and divers and track runners with bandages on my hands and elbows and sunscreen covering my body. The picture of me standing in front of the Olympic Swim Center at the Los Angeles Coliseum was frightening, wearing my yellow Weiner Factory sport shirt, white shorts, a baseball hat to hide under and bandages covering my hands and arms. But soon, I was beginning to mend. When it became time for yet one more extended hospitalization, I kindly asked Dr. Szydlo to find a doctor who could admit me to a private hospital where I could avoid the student probing, interviews and surveys that a teaching institution such as UCLA had to offer. I had been taken off the Ketanserin study due to a compassion clause. Since I was only getting sicker while on the experimental drug study, my name was pulled from the computer. We found out that I had indeed been on a placebo for months with no other helpful medications. Since I was deteriorating, I was allowed to go on the real medicine to see if I would benefit from it. I would become a testimonial for Ketanserin. I continued to be in the study on an individual basis. I soon had my original doctor, Donald Bernstein (who had referred me to Dr. Fan, the Rheumatologist) admit me into Tarzana Regional Medical Center, where I was to meet my next and current doctor, Jeffrey Galpin, an infectious disease specialist. Without wasting any time, the following morning, Dr. Galpin had a semi permanent Hickman Catheter inserted into my chest (heart) for long term intravenous antibiotic therapy. Right off the bat, nurses could not even line my veins up for an I.V., so this was a way to avoid the pain and misery of having my veins poked and re-poked, and it would allow me to get a long term dose of antibiotics in my body, to rid me of habitual osteomyolitis, a nasty effect of my Raynauds, the vascular phenomenon that was the onset of my illness, and a chronic problem.

The next morning when I awoke from the surgery, I felt like Don Corleone had visited me at the hospital and that I had been shot in the chest and neck. The line was now in and no one had to 'find my vein' or 'blow my vein' anymore. When Dr. Galpin came in to check on me, HE was on crutches as he had been plagued with polio just months before the vaccine was distributed. I said to him, "Are YOU my doctor?" and when he laughed, I knew that this was the beginning of a beautiful friendship.

After spending just eleven days this time at Tarzana Medical Hospital, Dr. Galpin sent me home with a new Home Care Program called HiCare Health. Gayle Grossman became my new I.V. nurse and newest of friends. She came by, plugged me into my meds, and taught Scott how to do it so that she could just leave several days of meds for me in the refrigerator at a time. Scott was good at hooking me up and administering intravenous antibiotics for the next two months and we both felt that by this time we had our honorary M.D.s. I could feel the bone infections subsiding and my pain being greatly relieved. Of course by now, my right hand was completely fused in a fist and was not of much use. My left hand only had two fingers which had not been infected by the osteomyolitis, so I had minimal function and use of my hands. People would ask me at the checkout line in the market if I had been in a burn accident. I learned to hide my hands in public as best as I could, never getting over the embarrassment of how ugly they had become.

Every once in a while, something would happen to cause me to look down at my hands or to take an extra long look at my face in the magnifying mirror and in a split second, I would be reminded of what had happened to me. I would remember the pain, the not knowing about my health and the disfigurement. I would regress back to a mentally painful and disturbing place. One of the unwelcome sensations that I have often experienced is that of the 'phantom limb.' You think your fingers are where they are not and you don't know where they are when you think you do. They get in the way or they drop something. It's a lousy feeling.

It would take a lot of energy and work to find that positive attitude that people always said I projected. I would have to take time and examine all kinds of experiences in my life; which battles to fight, when to stop raising my hand to volunteer, and when to jump into another new challenge. I would have to pull myself back to a healthy frame of mind, a place where I could strive for peace of mind and contentment in my life. Acknowledging my husband and all that he did for me, my family and friends who stayed by me and maintaining the network of supportive relationships became my new ADL.

The original hand specialist, Dr. Roy Meals, at UCLA had told me to come back and see him when I had been stable for five years. He would then see if there was a way to set my hands in a more permanent, but functional position. He operated on my hands in the fall of 1987 and they have been fused in the same position ever since.

Before being admitted to Tarzana Hospital, I had registered to take two art classes at the local community college. Having been a dancer my whole life, my creative juices needed a good outlet and I always liked drawing. But dance classes of any kind had been placed on the back burner for quite some time. Maybe art classes would get my hands moving and my brain stimulated. I spoke to the teacher, Mr. Alex Carrillo, from my hospital bed, explaining my life to him and asking him to hold my spot as I was to miss the beginning of the semester. I headed to class with a catheter in my chest and a smile on my face. Most of the kids in the class thought I was just another student, not an old, sick lady trying to mend a frustrated mind. I continued to take classes over the next five years in art, design, printmaking, drawing, life drawing, acrylic painting, watercolor, and even choreography. It was sort of like getting an AA in Art long after receiving my BA in Psychology and Dance, my MA in Dance-Movement Therapy and my Post Graduate Certification in Dance. I loved going back to school and the feelings of accomplishment that came along with hard work, determination, and dedication. I loved feeling productive and creative and I truly needed to, but I did miss the dancing, a lot! I learned so much from the wonderful art teachers at Pierce College. Mr. John Corbeil, my watercolor and acrylic teacher, not only taught me about art, color and composition, but about the importance of family. He had a ton of kids, all with cool names, like Teal and Piper, and always said that in his old age he wanted to be surrounded by his loving family. I was envious.

We decided to start our adoption research as the summer rolled around and right away found out some interesting information. We chose to move ahead with the Vista Del Mar Adoption Agency and began the workshop and orientation process. We received the Adoption Department PRELIMINARY INFORMATION FORM in late July, 1984 and returned it with its fee. Two adoption orientation meetings followed and then we took the 'Pathways to Parenthood' workshop. We were given many suggested reading lists, handouts, pamphlets, flyers and articles to read. We looked forward to the day our Home Study was approved.

We learned all about the procedure of adoption, how to deal with many various situations and what starting a family through adoption was truly about. We continued to learn through Vista Del Mar's Pathways program and were strongly suggested to go to infertility counseling as part of the application process. Since our reasons for adopting were very different than most perspective adoptive parents, we chose instead to go to family counseling for several sessions to discuss our feelings regarding adoption.

We met with a new counselor who did all the talking, about her! It was true; the old saying, that psychotherapy sessions are good for what ails the psychologist! We took her the video we had made with Dr. Carroll, our original psychiatrist from Westwood, that we had seen together early on when I was first diagnosed, for his teaching program at UCLA, regarding therapy with the chronically ill, for her review. She talked to us about our commitment to starting a family and the learning process involved in adoption. We were very committed to knowing as much as possible about the adoption process, legally, emotionally, and logically. We kept an open mind and let Vista Del Mar guide us though the adoption adaptation and information process. This was very different than going to a lawyer, finding a birth mother and receiving a child. This was learning about a lifetime process; we would always be as prepared and informed as possible. We discussed with the therapist the options of adopting a baby of a different race. We originally thought that it would be fine with us. We learned more about adoption and that adoption began the day you bring the baby home from the hospital (or wherever), not ending that day, as so many people think. We took a good long look at things like family, education and community and decided we were capable of taking a child of Caucasian or possibly American-Asian or mixed ethnicity decent. We thought that more children may be available that would need a home placement, if we expanded our ethnicity choices. We marked the category 'Newborn' on the application, which was considered to be 0-5 years old, and headed back to Vista feeling knowledgeable and confident that we had done as much as we could to prepare for this lifelong process. The counselor-social worker gave us the thumbs up to continue with Vista. One more step out of the way and on to the next.

A poem we received at one of the Pathway classes has remained our favorite after all these years:

> Once there were two women
> Who never knew each other
> One you do not remember
> The other you call mother
> Two different lives shaped to make yours one
> One became your guiding star
> The other became your sun.
> The first gave you life
> And the second taught you to live in it
> The first gave you a need for love
> And the second was there to give it.
> One gave you a nationality
> The other gave you a name
> One gave you the seed of talent
> The other gave you an aim.
> One gave you emotions

The other calmed your fears
One saw your first sweet smile
The other dried your tears.
One gave you up – it was all she could do
The other prayed for a child
And God led her straight to you.
And now you ask me through your tears,
The age-old question through the years,
Heredity or environment –
which are you a product of?
Neither my darling – neither
Just two different kinds of love.

Anonymous

We continued our workshop processes, informing my doctors that we needed medical and personal references for our adoption application and to inform those who would write those letters of our decision making process. The next formality was the Home Study visits. We began to get the house ready to be scrutinized and analyzed by complete strangers who would decide our fate as future parents. But quickly our hopes turned to grave despair as we were again to meet with our assigned social worker, Selma, in the Van Nuys office of Vista Del Mar, in the United Way building.

Expecting a routine meeting as part of the process, we were extremely shocked and disappointed when we were called into Selma's office. She informed us that on the basis of my having a 'life threatening' illness, that our application was denied. We were horrified and devastated. We would not be allowed to adopt a child through Vista. How could this be? We asked numerous questions. We reminded her that Vista had known since the very first day well over a year ago, that we came to the orientation meeting, that we were not like so many of the other perspective adoptive parents, that we had not been in infertility treatment for years. We were there because I had a condition that led to my being a 'guinea pig' for an experimental drug study at UCLA, that I had taken a drug that had not been and never was FDA approved and that my illness was in limbo and we didn't know how stable my health was just yet. We didn't know what effects the experimental drug may have had on my body. We weren't positive I could not have children of my own, but we were making preparations just the same. By the time of our denial, my health had stabilized.

My doctor's referral letters had gone unnoticed. Both Dr. Galpin and Dr. Szydlo had clarified my health status with high recommendations as to our ability to parent and live a long and fruitful life. My ambition to work and help others should have meant something. I was on the Medical and Educational committee for the Arthritis Foundation of Southern California as well as its Advisory Board for fundraising. I even taught their Self Help classes. Scott was a dedicated husband who was serving as the President of our own Universal Scleroderma Foundation. Why hadn't they read these letters and autobiographies? Why were they denying us our long time dream of becoming a family? Who had finalized these decisions? We were practically speechless when we departed the agency. I was truly forlorn. Several letters were sent to Vista as letters of recommendation. I found copies of three of them in my adoption file, two medical and one personal. If I had read them, I would pick us as adoptive parents!

Chapter Three

Hallmark of the Disease

Dear Vista Del Mar,

I would be very pleased to provide you with insight on Scleroderma and more specifically, Andrea Matis.

Scleroderma is a disease of connective tissue, the tissue which provides the structural framework of many parts of the body, including skin, blood vessels, joints, muscles, and internal organs such as the kidneys, lungs, heart, and digestive tract.

The hallmark of the disease is the excessive production of connective tissue, collagen. Collagen is a fibrous protein that can be thought of as the woven threads that make up a piece of cloth. It is the same protein that is essential for proper wound healing which often results in a shiny scar. In Scleroderma, too much collagen is produced and deposited in the skin and internal organs. This results in thickening and hardening of skin, as well as variable degrees of damage and dysfunction of the internal organs.

Approximately 100,000 to 300,000 people in the United States have Scleroderma. The disease has a global distribution and no race is excluded. Women get the disease three to five times more often then men, though men have a poorer prognosis. The peak period of onset of the disease is between 30 and 50 years of age. The cause of the disease is unknown. It is known, however, that it is neither contagious nor hereditary.

The thick hardened skin of Scleroderma may

restrict the motion of the underlying bones and joints. The hands may become partially bent as a result of flexion fractures.

Cold may temporarily reduce circulation in the fingers, causing them to blanch or turn bluish. Collagen deposits in blood vessels may further restrict blood flow to the fingers, sometimes resulting in open sores, or ulcerations. Circulation in the fingers can be improved by keeping warm, wearing gloves, learning biofeedback and by taking various drugs.

Involvement of the esophagus, the muscular tube which propels food from the mouth to the stomach, results in abnormal swallowing. Patients may get a sticking sensation in the chest or heartburn. Simple measures like taking antacids or drugs, and not eating late in the evening, can alleviate these symptoms.

The most serious complication of Scleroderma is "renal crisis", which is a sudden rise in blood pressure followed by kidney failure. Until 1978, this complication was nearly 100% fatal within six months. Research led to the development of a drug which cut the mortality rate by a full 50%. Fortunately, patients who do not develop this complication within the first three years of developing the disease generally do not develop renal crisis at all. After having the disease for five years, the chances for developing renal crisis are nil.

Cardiac involvement can result in heart failure or disturbances in normal heart rhythm. Heart attacks are <u>not</u> associated with Scleroderma. Though cardiac involvement may result in death, most cardiac manifestations can be treated with drugs.

Patients may have involvement of the lungs which can result in shortness of breath with exertion. Though lung involvement may be slowly progressive over many years, it may remain stable, or even improve to some extent.

Though Scleroderma remains an incurable disease, many of its manifestations can be treated and alleviated. The rate of the progression of the disease is quite variable and cannot be predicted. Certainly, patients who have considerable involvement of the kidneys, heart or lungs at the time of diagnosis have a worse prognosis. The most rapid rate of progression occurs in the first three years, after which the rate plateaus, or proceeds much more slowly over many years. Patients with minimal internal organ involvement can live a normal lifespan.

Andrea Matis has had Scleroderma for over three years. Her skin involvement is mild. Her fingers have developed flexion contractures which limit her joint motion. She does not have any ulcers at this time. Though her fingers cannot be straightened, the problem has not prevented her from excelling as an artist in the drawing classes she attends regularly. People with hand dysfunction become very resourceful, learning to do old activities in new ways, sometimes with the assistance of home-made or commercially available adaptive devices.

Her symptoms due to mild esophageal involvement have been virtually eliminated with treatment. Since she has had the disease for longer than three years without the development of renal crisis, the chances of her getting this in the future are remote. Andrea has no evidence of any cardiac involvement.

Andrea has only mild lung involvement, detected only by sophisticated pulmonary function testing. Her lung involvement has remained stable over the past three years without evidence of any progression. Perhaps she has been benefited by her previous work as a professional dancer and aerobics teacher, which strengthened her pulmonary and cardiovascular system prior to getting Scleroderma. She still swims and does other exercises without serious limitations.

At this time, she is being treated with only two drugs. She takes Zantac 150 mg twice daily to reduce the acid production by her stomach, thereby relieving her heartburn. She also takes Nifedipine 20 mg three times a day for improvement of her finger circulation.

As head of the UCLA Scleroderma Clinic and someone who does research on this disease, I have gained considerable expertise in treating patients with this disease. Despite my experience, I cannot predict the patient's course and prognosis with 100% certainty. I can say, however, that Andrea Matis has a mild disease and a good prognosis. She has passed the most crucial stage of this disease - the first three years. Her course will remain stable or progress much more slowly. In my opinion, she has a good chance of having a normal lifespan and a very good quality of life.

I know that she is psychologically prepared to be a parent. Her only potential limitation in parenting a child is her altered hand function. Her beautiful drawings are a testimony of her ability to overcome some limitations. I think she is very capable of parenting an infant or toddler with part-time assistance at home. I do not believe her disease will have any adverse effects on a child that she will be parenting, particularly in view of her great desire to do so.

I do hope you seriously consider the Matis family as prospective adoptive parents. I know they will raise wonderful children.

Sincerely yours,

Lillian Szydlo, M.D.
Assistant Professor
UCLA School of Medicine

     By the time we had walked to the parking lot at the valley office of Vista Del Mar, and got into the car, we realized we were fuming with anger. What were we going to do? How would we face this dilemma? We drove to my parent's house in Tarzana to tell them the situation. They were so excited about the adoption process and the potential of becoming grandparents. I needed to tell them what happened and also felt like I needed to get some love and support from my own mom and dad. My father was furious. As a philanthropist of mega proportions, he had been a long time supporter of a subsidiary company that aided the Vista Del Mar Adoption Agency. He walked into the back room, his office, and came out with a phone number. He told Scott to call and speak to the higher ups at Vista. He told us NOT to give up, and to be aggressive and firm with our ideals.

     And then another medical reference…

Dear Vista Del Mar,

     Thank you for asking me to comment about Andrea Matis, her illness, how it might affect adopting a child, and the obligation that you obviously command to both the child and to the parents in placing these children in adequate homes, and I agree that it is a complex and awesome responsibility.

First let me tell you what Scleroderma is, which is what Andrea Matis is suffering from. Scleroderma is one of a broad spectrum of what are called collagen vascular illnesses that also relate to rheumatoid arthritis, to a disease called lupus erythematosus, to other diseases like ankylosing spondylitis, and inflammatory bowel disease. It is an illness that is capricious and yet predictable in a sense that if one begins with a severe form of the disease, which progresses over several years very, very rapidly, then this individual who has this type of illness would typically continue along that same curve with the same type of accelerated deterioration.

Andrea has a disease that affects the skin and connective tissue of her hands and somewhat of her lower legs as well. She has had it now for several years. It has been slow to progress, and in fact, over the last six months to a year has appeared to be perfectly stable. There is every hope, although certainly no guarantee, that the disease will stay fairly much intact in the form in which it now exists, that is, that she has some limitations of her hands and of her lower extremities, but walks, can do ballet, dance, can do everything that she needs to do: she is able to write, paint, cook, and is absolutely self sufficient.

Andrea, herself, is a dynamic, bright, energetic woman, who certainly will make a wonderful mother. She is the type of individual who, given the opportunity and with her handicap will more than overcompensate with loving care and dedication. Her disease, because it has been very slow, and in fact appears to be at this moment almost in remission, although again, there are no guarantees, should not hinder her from becoming a mother and having the ability to spend the years in raising a child to maturity. She has a supportive, loyal husband. The two of them together offer much that many other couples do not offer. In addition, they have the special benefit of knowing illness, knowing health, having a reality system that would benefit any child or group of children. Overall, I see no hesitation on my part in recommending that Andrea be offered the opportunity and the privilege of having a child to adopt, and I see it as a blessing for the child to obtain this quality of parenting. The disease itself, as stated, cannot be guaranteed, but no more can be guaranteed of anyone who right now walks this earth that a devastating disease could not strike them. Certainly, there will be some limitation, but that limitation is minimal, and in no way will decrease the quality of care offered to that child.

Can the disease get worse? Certainly it is possible. Will it stay in check? Certainly there is some evidence at this point. Her years, either way, would be toward 20-30 years certainly before, at this rate, there would be any major chance for devastating sequelae, and I think certainly the next 10-20 years look very good in terms of her health staying relatively stable.

If there are any further questions, please do not hesitate to call.

Yours truly,

Jeffrey Galpin, M.D.

And on a lighter note, a more personal referral came from our best friend since college...

Dear Vista Del Mar,

I am writing in response to your request for a

reference in relation to Andrea and Scott Matis.

Andrea and Scott have been my closest friends for 11 years. We've been through college, graduate school, world travels, home buying, career changes, illness, traumas, and many, many happy times together. I am thrilled to be used as a reference for them as potential parents, because I know them individually, and as a couple, better than almost anyone in their lives.

As a couple, they are very closely bonded. They have a great deal of mutual respect for each other, and are very good friends. I feel they are truly a couple who enjoy, love, and like each other very much. They communicate well (better than any other married couple I know), and consult each other on any decision that will effect them, their marriage, their future. They do live up to today's ideal of accepting one's mate for who they are, and supporting the marriage above all else. The only thing that could make their relationship and lives more complete would be a family of their own.

Andrea and Scott both come from very closely knit and affectionate families. They have healthy relationships with their siblings, parents, cousins. Because of their family-oriented upbringing, all children born into the families are loved, attended to, given enough guidance, but are allowed to become independent people in their own right. In other words, a child to Andrea and Scott would of course contribute to each of their individual fulfillment, but will be respected and considered as someone with its own needs, priorities and self-esteem.

On a lighter note, Andrea and Scott have endless energy and interests to share with a child, a beautiful home, a great dog—all the things that make a normal kid happy and satisfied. If I were a child in need of a home, theirs would be a dream come true.

Please don't hesitate to contact me with further questions.

Leslie Williams

We returned home and tried to calm down. When we got to our home in Woodland Hills, Scott rallied and phoned one of the directors at the adoption agency. He explained in detail what had just happened after over a year and a half of our dedicated involvement with Vista. In what we thought was an appeasement, we were told that we would hear back within a week regarding our application. I truly thought that call would never come, and if it did, it would be bad news for the Matises.

A week later, Mr. Reuben Pannor phoned. This was a man who was an expert in adoption and was on the board of the adoption agency. We had seen him on 'Oprah' and had read articles by him. Later, we would attend workshops with him. He told Scott that we were back on a waiting list and able to continue with our Home Study. It sounded like an appeasement and we were still highly doubtful. It sounded like we had been given the runaround. I just didn't believe it and so we agreed that by my 33rd birthday (almost another year away), if we had not made it to the top three on the waiting list, we would then seek out other methods of adoption, including other agencies and lawyers. We had learned plenty at this point and could now be open to other ways to start our family! We rescheduled the Home Study visits and we also demanded a new social worker. This was when we met Harvey.

Harvey was our savior; a nice, mellow man, a little older than we were and very understanding of the situation we had been through. Harvey was very easy going, compassionate, and empathetic. He came to evaluate our house on Ninfa Court in Woodland Hills: the house we loved and could not believe we lived in, all custom remodeled with Koa wood from Hawaii, stained glass and maple inlaid cabinetry. The backyard reached back forever, with a basketball court and a beautiful rolling hillside. We held my brother Joel's wedding there, after which the entire family held hands together during "Hands Across America." We knew that we would have to install a pool fence, though we didn't know it would eventually become an ad in the *Los Angeles Times* for a pool fence company. Our backyard looked so lovely. Aside from that, we were good perspective adoptive parents. He thought our home was a wonderful place to raise a child. We loved that home. We sailed through our home study and then the waiting began.

In the meantime, I made some other moves thinking that all would not go as planned. I went to my Ob-Gyn and got a referral to a fertility specialist in Beverly Hills. Dr. Donald Adler had African fertility masks on his walls and women lining up to use his restroom. The testing began. Blood work, sexually transmitted diseases, allergies to Scott, you name it. Oh, of course, the sperm count was first and foremost, and of course, it was as high as can be. Or, as we said, one hundred million and counting. So, the rest was up to me now.

My girlfriend, Margie, who had driven me so many times to the hospital and tests at UCLA once again, accompanied me to my next fertility test, the hysterosalpingogram. The fertility radiologist's office was directly behind Dr. Adler's office in Beverly Hills. They were going to dilate my cervix, shoot some dye up into my fallopian tubes and see by x-ray, that all was clear for sperm to reach my eggs. They warned me the dilation may cause cramping, but that it wouldn't take too long. They even gave me pain medication to deal with it. I lay on the table with my knees up in the air, "Is this the cramping you told me about? Because it really hurts."

"We are having a problem getting the tube with the die into your cervix. You need to go to Dr. Adler's office and have them dilate you and then come back for the test."

"You mean now?"

And so Margie marched me across the back driveway in the heart of Beverly Hills in my patient gown to get my cervix dilated. Now that was some nasty cramping! Thank goodness I had taken a pain reliever. Then we walked back to the radiologist's office, the dye went straight in and my tubes were cleared for take off. It was then and there that we found out that my cervical entrance to my uterus simply was way too tight and that I had probably wasted years using birth control because most likely I would have never gotten pregnant. Another step was out of the way. This made way for the next solution, artificial insemination. The reason for the cervical tightness was not exactly clear. It could have been that I was a DES baby (diethylstilbestrol - my mother had taken it to prevent miscarriages when she was pregnant with me) or Scleroderma, no one knew for sure. Artificial insemination by husband (AIH) was our next step.

For ten months I would take my temperature, to check for ovulation, drive to Beverly Hills for ultrasounds, get artificially inseminated with Scott's sperm, and pray that my health would maintain so that I wouldn't need to go on any medications during this whole process. In August of 1986, I found out that I was pregnant. I was to remain on bed rest with no major activity or exercise. Four weeks later, I started to spot. I went back to Dr. Adler's office for another ultrasound. There was no heartbeat. Scott and I cried and cried. We got through the Jewish High Holidays with comments like, "It wasn't meant to be," and "You can try again," but we were distraught and didn't want to hear anyone's commentary. We went to therapy and mourned our loss. I mended and held my breath awaiting news from Vista Del Mar.

It was Christmas time of 1986. My health was as good as ever; well as good as it had been in four years. My hands were still bent and contracted, but I had learned to live with that by now. Sometimes people didn't even notice! Dealing with the position my hands were in was what I referred to as 'leverage'. If I couldn't hold something one way, I balanced it between my fingers or any other way I could manage. I had a unique way of holding a pen. My teeth became quite useful even though, Mr. Corbeil, my painting teacher, would constantly yell at me for using them to open paint tubes and eventually I did chip them over time. Holding, eating, writing, and cooking utensils were a challenge, as was using paint brushes and carrying canvases to my art classes. I purchased padded utensil holders to use on my forks, toothbrushes and paintbrushes. Art kept my spirits up and my creative juices churning. I had amazing teachers in all of my courses at Pierce College in Woodland Hills. I wasn't dancing, but I was creating and truly enjoying it. And I had joined a gym and was beginning to move my body again. I was asked to interview for an article for the Arthritis Foundation in a local paper and to do a fundraiser for the Universal Scleroderma Foundation by selling my watercolors at a Rotary show in Encino. I had been to New York to meet with a scleroderma fundraising group there to work together, and to Chicago, as a patient advisor for a new information pamphlet for the Arthritis Foundation. I was busy educating others and helping to raise funds for PSS. Then after over a year, the call came.

I remember being in my bedroom upstairs. A painted 'copy' of the mural from the local Saks Fifth Avenue with waterfalls and lush plants was on my headboard wall. We never had a headboard as I was always afraid I would bang my fingers against it and cut myself, resulting in a possible infection. Our bed was raised on cinder blocks for my reflux and I climbed up on it when the phone rang. It was Harvey. My stomach came up in my throat, not an unusual feeling for me with my esophagus! This time, it was for a different reason. "I have a birth mother in my office. I want to know if you want to be considered to be adoptive parents for her child." Did I hear him correctly?

"For real? Say that again", I replied.

"She is about eight months pregnant, give or take. She's not quite sure. You are on the top three of our waiting list…should I submit your profile for her to review?"

"Yes, yes, yes!" I could not believe it. I had to call Scott immediately. "Give her our file!"

"You know she gets to read three profiles and decides who she wants to interview. This by no way means she will select you to meet with." Harvey was being gentle with me.

"By all means, give her our profile; let her consider us…thank you so much!"

And so the first call came and went and in my shock I called Scott at the Wiener Factory to tell him the

59

astonishing news. I could barely speak. My heart was racing. It was beating so loud in my head that I thought the whole world could hear it. My brain was in a fog. Scott was elated. We had not been appeased. We had actually made it to the top of the waiting list. Now if this birth mother could just realize that we were the people she was looking for!

Two days before Christmas, Harvey phoned us again. We had been considered along with two other couples to be adoptive parents. But the good news was that she had chosen US to interview. I held my breath and my tongue through Christmas dinner with the Matis family, not wanting to jinx anything. My mother was a very superstitious woman and had ingrained this in my head over the years, not to say anything before it happened. We had not told any of the Matises of our two year involvement with Vista Del Mar. We had not wanted to be questioned without knowing all the answers. We told no one of the upcoming interview. While Scott's sister talked of adopting a baby from the biggest adoption attorney in Los Angeles, we kept quiet and ate our meal. We didn't know what would happen, if the birth mother would want us to raise her baby. Maybe she would meet us and not even like us. There I was, with bent, deformed hands and a pretty poor health record. Why would she possibly pick us? She could choose younger, healthier and certainly more affluent parents than us! It was going to be her choice.

We waited until December 26th and headed to the West Los Angeles offices of the Vista Del Mar Adoption Agency. I was wearing my Kelley green skirt and sweater outfit. I really liked how I looked and it made me feel good and ready for the first meeting. I was wondering where I would put my hands to hide them from sight. No pockets were always the challenge. What would she think of us, our behavior together, and our sense of humor? Then Scott and I had a simultaneous thought in the parking lot on National Boulevard. "What if she looks like Ilene?" a mutual friend who's physical countenance was most unappealing in appearance. And then our laughter ignited. Having released our tension, we opened the car doors to head into Vista. Our fate was now in a stranger's hands. The staircase looked endless as we walked across the parking lot.

We walked into Harvey's office. "Katherine is in the other room. She has a different social worker handling her case. He will sit with us and we will all be together for the initial meeting". Harvey was gentle as always.

In walked another man and a young, tall, slim blonde who appeared to have eaten a basketball. "This is Katherine. And this is Harvey." Another Harvey, how weird. So we had two Harvey's watching over us. I shook her hand with my left hand, as I always did (the better of the two) and Scott introduced both of us to Katherine. We all sat down. I was nervous, but so excited. We started to talk. Two hours later, I knew. I knew that this was a match made in heaven. That this union was meant to be. B'shert was the Yiddish term my mom had taught me, and this is exactly what it meant. All those cliché terms would come to pass. We asked questions. She asked questions.

What are your hobbies?

Dance.

Dance. Oh my god, she's a dancer. She's the gypsy girl I always thought I was. She traveled. She was from the valley.

Scott stared at her, "Harpo?"

I looked at Scott in stunned silence. We all did. It appeared Scott knew her. She had worked for Scott at the Wiener Factory several years ago for a very brief time. This was a secret we had always kept from everyone. The astonishing and unlikely coincidence was simply too odd to try to explain to anyone, well, except maybe my sister who knew every detail of the adoption process from day one. Good Old Miriam, my best friend and confidant in life.

As Katherine told us her story, her life in Europe and her pregnancy, we realized what it was she was looking for. She told us that upon her return to the United States from Spain, she was referred to a lawyer in Santa Barbara to help with the adoption placement. She met with him and was dealing with him for several months when he found a couple who wanted to adopt her baby. It turned out that they didn't want to meet her. They didn't want to ever have a relationship with her after the birth of the baby. They didn't want to let her know how the baby was doing, send pictures in the future or keep her informed of what would happen when the child grew up.

Katherine was heartsick. She felt all alone in the world and this certainly was not what she wanted. Her situation felt as bleak as ours had at the time of our rejection. She denied this couple and asked to be referred to someone else to help her. This was when the lawyer researched and found Vista Del Mar and this is why she was so late in her pregnancy when she got there. She wanted an open adoption, which was the way Vista preferred. She wanted to know how her child would be six months later. Five years later. She wanted to receive pictures and to send them. She wanted to write her special letter for the teenager to read someday. It certainly all made sense to us. Who wouldn't want these things? Of course we would want to know where she was and how she was doing after the birth, in six months, and in five years. We verbally agreed to an open adoption immediately. We couldn't imagine her not being in our lives after the baby was born. She was a dynamic woman with a heart of gold. A spiritual artist and lover of mankind. One of the most good hearted people I'd ever met and I knew all this in less than 2 hours.

Now, we all wanted to know more about each other. What were her circumstances? What had she eaten during the pregnancy? Were we religious? Would the baby be raised in a spiritual home? The energy was staggering. The room was ignited. It was as if we had all known each other for years. "Would you be able to pay for my birthing classes? It's thirty five dollars."

"Of course, what else do you need?" We began to work out logistics. How do we get registered at West Hills Humana Hospital for the delivery? What day? Can we come? We planned to meet several days later in a coffee shop in the valley to talk without counselors around and to make further arrangements. This is when we discovered the story of the 'name'.

We met Katherine at Marie Calendars in Northridge. We continued our conversation from a few days earlier, and made plans to register Katherine for her delivery at West Hills Humana Hospital, and learned about her living situation. She had been living with her aunt, one of her mother's sisters, since her return from Europe. She had been back in California for about 3 months. She left her Swedish boyfriend, Anders, in Madrid when it was confirmed that she was pregnant. Her suspicions had told her that she was pregnant for quite a while, but the medical clinics kept telling her that she was not. Finally, an ultrasound proved her to be five months pregnant and Anders and she decided it would be best for her to give birth and place the baby for adoption in the United States. They were not ready to get married and according to Katherine, after having numerous fathers and stepfathers, she wasn't jumping into any quick marriage for convenience decision making. She could not do that to the new baby, or to herself.

As we talked in the coffee shop, we realized we had so many similarities. We began to feel like soul sisters having led parallel, but also very different lives. What I could not believe, was that we were the same age. Most birth mothers were much younger than I, and it felt so wonderful to be on so many of the same wavelengths. Casually, yet with immense curiosity, we asked Katherine if she had a name picked out for the baby.

"Seren" she said. "It's from a book, the *Road Less Traveled*. Do you know it? I got it from the word 'serendipity'. It means 'the faculty for making providential discoveries by accident.'" An unexpected, but most welcomed gift.

"I always wondered what that word meant. You mean something good comes from an unplanned incident."

"Yes, and that is what this is all about," Katherine looked pensive, but strong her in choice for adoption. She had weighed the various outcomes of her predicament and knew she was doing the right thing. She conveyed to us that she was no longer interested in interviewing any other families and that she was so pleased that we had come into her unstable life.

That was so strange! The name Scott and I were thinking of for the middle name was Zaron. Kind of sounds the same. It was for a good friend and we just liked the name so much we thought we'd use it. The first name was unmistakably going to be Bruce. We almost didn't have a choice. Actually, not at all! Everyone assumed we would name our first child for Bruce Springsteen. Springsteen concerts and albums had gotten us through our dating years and early marriage. He was there for us through thick and thin. Of course, we also had my Aunt Bea, my father's sister who had recently passed away from cancer, to be memorialized. We even had plans for the birth announcement to say "Born in the USA" as its caption, a Springsteen album title. Besides the Wiener Factory coincidence, we had arrived at our second psychic moment, the name.

We had picked a day to register at the hospital, January 8th at nine in the morning, exchanged financials and headed on our way. New Year's was coming and we had so much to celebrate. You never know how sure something is, but we were pretty darn sure that this was going to happen. We were so sure that no one involved was going to have a change of mind. Sometimes you just know a good thing when it happens. Maybe I had my MomMom's intuition. Maybe I was the psychic!

I could not keep this secret from one person any longer. It was time to call my sister, my best friend in the whole world. "Mir, can you meet Scott and me for lunch? We need to talk to you about something." The last time I had made such an ominous call to her was for quite different reasons. In the darkest time of my illness we called Miriam and asked her to meet us for lunch. We were going on vacation and wanted to ask her if she would accept our 'inheritance' (be what it may) if anything were to happen to us while we were traveling. This time we wanted to tell her that she would no longer reap our riches, that we were going to have a child that would take over that role in our lives. She had once even offered to surrogate a baby for us when things looked very bad. We met at the Ritz restaurant on Pico Boulevard. "We're adopting a baby. We've been chosen by a birth mother. You're going to be an aunt. And if you would, could you please be the godmother?"

"Oh yes!" She exclaimed and we had to keep reminding her to close her mouth while she ate her lunch that day! She couldn't have been happier for us. Later in time, all of her good friends would come to play with Bruce and some even to baby sit for us.

On January 4th, I asked Scott if he thought it was time we should tell his parents about the adoption. They knew nothing over the past few years and since I was positive we would be parents by the end of the month, I thought we should tell them. We wouldn't want anyone to have a heart attack from shock when we brought our new baby home. By only telling a few people along the way, we hoped that would keep our Karma in the best place and not do that jinx thing my mom warned us about. We also knew that there would have been a series of endless unanswerable questions along the way that we thought best left that way for the time being. We phoned Scott's parents in Las Vegas that evening and made his mom swear not to tell ANYONE until we told her that is was okay to do so. We simply had been through so much the first four years of our marriage that we didn't want anything to go wrong at this point. Scott's parents were in shock, but also sounded extremely delighted. They promised to keep the secret as long as we said, so that our luck and good karma would continue. Scott's dad also had a thing for jinxing. As superstitious as they were, they understood what we were asking. It was a good thing that Katherine's questionable due date arrived on the early side.

I had made arrangements with West Hills Humana Hospital in the Valley to take Katherine there on January eighth to pre-register her, take a tour and find out how to arrange the payments for a non family member. We were taken by surprise when the phone rang at six in the morning that same day. Another psychic moment between us! Katherine's aunt was calling to say Katherine had been having pains and they were already at the hospital. Then Katherine got on the phone and said she was confident it was false labor and that they would be sending her home soon, but she wanted to put us on notice. We tried to go back to sleep, but just lay in bed with our eyes and hearts wide open. Within the hour, the phone rang again. Indeed, it was the real thing. We were to get to the hospital and officially admit Katherine immediately.

Arriving at West Hills that morning was like a dream. We floated into the admissions office and officially registered Katherine while she lay in the Labor Room. We were led to the Maternity Ward and then we too went into the Labor Room. There she was. A woman we had barely met and barely knew, cracking jokes in between her cringing and breathing. We met her aunt, with whom she had been staying since her return to the states, and her birth coach from her Lamaze class. It was like one big happy family. We chatted like we had known each other for years, not days. After a few hours, around eleven a.m., Katherine was experiencing greater pain. It was then that she asked for Scott to leave. If only we had known her longer. We so would have both loved to be in the birthing room with her. But she just wasn't comfortable enough for that, and of course, we understood. Several hours later, about one o'clock, Katherine asked for just her aunt to be in the room with her and I regretfully left for a little lunch.

The nurse asked if we were ready to take the baby home.

It was then that Scott and I had a reality check. Did we have diapers, undershirts, bottles and most important, did we have the car seat? Oh my god! We were so unprepared. We weren't even legally ready to take the baby home without a car seat! Quickly, we went to the pay phone and called my folks. Oh, the cell phone would have been a great benefit in those days. Could they please go to the store today and get everything we needed to bring the baby home tomorrow? I have heard over and over since that call that it was the happiest time in my parents' life. What they wouldn't have done or paid that day! They arrived at the hospital several hours later after their long shopping spree at J.C. Penney's with a trunk full of items. You name it, they had bought it. They were beaming from ear to ear. They joined us and the other prospective parents in the waiting room. I felt like I was in one of those old movies, where the father waits in the other room and then after the baby is born, they get to see the baby. Only now we were all dads. Time ticked by slowly. My parents made themselves at home and were soon talking with another older couple. It seemed that they were friends and that they too were awaiting the birth of a grandchild at the exact same time. We still run into those people and we talk about that miraculous day that we spent in the waiting room together.

At 5:07 pm, on January 8th, the nurse came out. It was the same birthday as Elvis Presley and David Bowie: was music in his future? Katherine had given birth. We were parents

When, when can we see? Is it a boy like she felt it was? Ten fingers and ten toes? Weight? And most important of all, how was Katherine doing?

All was well. He was a 7 lb. 11 oz. baby boy. Happy, healthy and screaming his bloody head off! We were escorted to the nursery to look through the glass. On our introspective walk down the hall, we passed Katherine being wheeled to her room. I will never forget her face. My mom will never forget her face. Scott will never forget her face. She couldn't disguise her feelings this time. No jokes were coming out. She looked sad and worried. Had she done the right thing? Who were we to take the baby from her? I could see the pain in her eyes. This was the hardest thing she had ever done in her life, and we all knew it.

My brain shifted gears as we soon approached the nursery window. "That one, that one is ours!" His tiny blue hat and our giant buttons that said, "It's a boy." My face hurt from smiling so much. Scott had tears in his eyes. We were a family! My mother wore her giant baby blue button which read, "Ask me about my grandchild."

Bruce was still screaming when we arrived to watch him through the window. There was a man in the waiting room who asked, "Which one is yours?"

I pointed to our baby, "That one!" I said. "The one with the great lungs!" He turned to me and asked what we were going to name him. "Bruce", I said.

"Bruce who?" he asked.

"Bruce Matis," I replied and he said, "Good, I want to know that baby's name, so when he is famous I can say, I saw him screaming in the nursery the day he was born!" And of course, we all knew he would be famous some day. All new parents know that about their newborn babies.

The next item on the agenda was taking the roll of dimes out, yes dimes, that we were advised to take with us the day we adopt a baby so that we could make phone calls to relatives and friends. And so the calls began. If we heard it once, "Are you naming him Bruce?" we must have heard it a million times that day. It's a good thing we picked that name, because everyone else had picked it for us, whether or not they knew before the call that we were adopting a baby.

Congratulations were in order over and over. Scott's mom was so glad that she could tell everyone about the adoption now! Scott's sister said, "What? What are you talking about? I can't believe it! When do you come home?" Everyone was so happy for us. We were overjoyed.

On January 9th, 1987, we were to take our new baby boy home. He was twenty three hours old. I wanted to bring Katherine something, a gift. But I didn't know what. Flowers were for sick people and I didn't like them anyway, slowly wilting. They always reminded me of being sick in the hospital. And what would she do with balloons? I carefully looked through my jewelry box and picked a gold bracelet to give her. It felt right to give her something valuable of mine as a gift. There obviously was no gift that could come close to the one she was giving us, but I wanted to give her something special that she could have for a long time. It had been kind of like trading baskets in basketball. We felt like we were even. It took me a long time to realize that as much as we knew Katherine had done for our lives, that we had made her life stable and secure as well. I shot a basket, and then she shot a basket. The score was tied. We were soul sisters now.

The day after Bruce's birth, from Katherine's hospital room, Harvey escorted us back to the nursery. On the way he told us that is was the first time in fifteen years that he was placing a Caucasian baby from a birth mother to an adoptive family in the hospital. As a social worker, he had mainly placed international adoptions in recent years. He was thrilled with the situation. He also guided us through Katherine's situation with gentleness. He wanted to make sure that she was OK with her decision. It was a difficult choice for her and although we all felt assured that she would accept it over time, it was still very painful. He wanted to make sure we understood that we would be in contact with her, pictures would be exchanged and that we were to be supportive of her feelings along the way. What else would we be? We walked into the nursery. The nurses were almost as excited as we were. None of them had had EVER placed a baby for adoption while working at that hospital. They were asking so many questions. Then they found out, I hadn't changed a diaper since I was an eighteen year old babysitter! How do I make formula? Nail clippers? Me? I couldn't even cut my own nails! That's what salons were for. And then the baby was handed to me for the first time.

Katherine had been taken off the maternity floor at her request and was on a surgical floor. Walking into her room that day was one of the hardest things I have ever done. What was I going to say to her? There were no words that could express how we felt. The situation was so very bittersweet. This was the hardest thing Katherine had ever done in her life. We knew that. Yet, she knew that it was the most wonderful thing that ever happened in ours.

Serendipity indeed. Her face was full of mixed emotions. We hugged and hugged. We thanked her over and over for the gift of life that she was sharing with us. And she thanked us for helping her at this time in her life. Then we said our goodbyes with plans to meet in a few weeks before she headed back to Europe. She said she had a gift she wanted to leave with me for when Bruce got older. It was a native Swedish ornament, a spring tree. Since Bruce was half Swedish, conceived in Spain and born in California, it was just one of his heritages to keep. With mixed emotions, we said our goodbyes. We planned to meet at Serenia Park in Woodland Hills in two weeks. At that time, Katherine would give us a letter for Bruce and the Swedish arbor keepsake. Of course, the name of the park was perfect for Katherine as everything between us was falling into place, even the name of a park!

I picked up my newborn son in the hospital. I stared into his tiny baby face. His eyes were wandering around, trying to focus. They were navy blue. My girlfriend Leslie from college had always told me that I always said I wanted a baby with blue eyes and blonde hair, but I knew I would never get that, Scott and I both having brown hair and brown eyes. Well, Leslie also told me I could always get what I wanted. Here he was. The most beautiful newborn I had ever seen. His tiny fingers grasping mine. His little blue knit hat. His huge mouth screaming. Now what? The nurse showed me how to hold him, "Support his head and neck," she said. "Hold the bottle like this," and she elevated the bottom of the bottle upright.

Scott was holding his breath waiting for his turn. "Hey Bruce!" Scott said. And then and there his name was official. We were given a form for the picture they took in the hospital to order later. We were taking pictures for ourselves, with the nurse, the three of us, putting him in the car, his first time in a car seat. We were given a bag of baby goodies. Tiny little scissors, mini diapers, a nose squeegee thingy, and samples of formula. It was time to take our son home.

We called and asked my parents to come over. "Show me how to feed him, Mom," I said. Of course, there was no putting him down. I held him, Scott held him, my mom held him, and my dad held him. We walked him around his new home, up to his little bedroom with scleroderma garage sale furniture. We walked him out in the nice big backyard, around the pool and back to the basketball court. Maybe he would go to Lakers' games with us someday? Gladys and her new adopted Springer Spaniel sister, BJ, sat by my feet every time I fed him. If his car seat was on the dining table with him sleeping; they sat by the table and protected him. Scott and I looked at each other. We had the story of a lifetime in our eyes. Who would come over first? When can we take him to the mall? What would be his favorite games and toys? Now, my girlfriend, Cindy, could give us that shower she wanted to so badly!

Four days later, friends came to visit. Vicki, whose little boy was three at the time, trimmed his razor sharp little nails for me and her husband, Ron, gave us the best advice we would ever get regarding parenting. Advice we continued to give to everyone we knew who had a baby after us. Ronnie said, and I quote, "Here is the best advice I can give you...never listen to anyone else's advice!" and that was it. It stuck forever.

Katherine and I were connected in so many ways. We met a few weeks later, just Katherine and I, on a greenish brown hillside in barren Serenia Park. We talked. She told me that it was not going to work out for Anders and her after all. She was not returning to Europe. She would make her way right here in Southern California. She said it was a very tough few weeks and apologized for not having a note to keep for Bruce or the Midsummer Tree. She would send those as soon as she got settled in her new life. We held each other as if we would never let go and then the time came for two mothers to part and go on with their separate lives.

Chapter Four

Celebrating Life

We began raising Bruce and celebrating life as a family. We took so many pictures of him. We wrote to him in his blue and white baby book.

Dear Bruce Zaron,

You are the most special baby in the world. I love you and will care for you with all my heart and soul.

I love you,

Mom

We kept track of his vaccinations and put the Rolling Stone cover with Bruce Springsteen on it in the keepsake folder along with his Astrological Forecast, "the amusements you desire should be practical." Our families gathered to witness his circumcision and to welcome him into the Jewish faith. He had a Brit Milah Ceremony in our home on Ninfa Court with its beautiful Koa wood walls and stained glass windows. Scott's brother, Uncle Alan, was sweating bullets as he held Bruce and the Moyle performed his skilled task. In my winter white wool pants and matching silk blouse, the joke of the day was, "You look great. Lost all the baby weight already."

Bruce grew and smiled and laughed with us. Twice a year we had agreed to mail pictures to Katherine. But somehow I never sent her the best ones. I didn't want her to feel pained when she saw how beautiful he was. I wanted to ease her difficulty in giving him up for adoption. I wanted her life to move on and for her to be happy. We started to write letters and later promised to always let each other know about our lives. Harvey would call us or write us or forward things to us and keep us abreast of her whereabouts and how she was doing. Originally, we only communicated through Vista Del Mar and both Harveys. They would forward our letters to each other. Then, after time, we asked if we could remove the middle-man and just write to each other directly. We would keep our addresses current from then on. We knew Katherine was having a hard time. She never returned to Europe to be with Anders. They had broken up. She was on her own all alone in California. She kept her secret from her mother, as did her aunt. She moved from friend to friend and house to house. She wasn't there the day we had the Brit for Bruce. Later we would give him a Mikvah in the Pacific Ocean at the Malibu Colony and finalize his conversion to Judaism. She would have loved to have seen that. In what would be the first of many cards and letters that Katherine would send to us, Katherine began by sending a beautiful card that read,

SURELY A STAR DANCED IN THE HEAVENS...
ON THE DAY YOU WERE BORN

To this she added by hand,

2-26-87

To Seren (Bruce)...
Who warms my heart
melting the ice from
The long Winter's time
my tear flows
freely and knowingly
from my soul

76

~ Serenaid ~

For wherever I have walked
You have walked with me.
And when I soar
You soar beside me.
I love you Seren
    -Katherine

Then, in April the letter came that Katherine's social worker had told her to write to Bruce so that one day in the future, he may understand her choices.

April 28, 1987

Dearest Seren/Bruce,

Just one more of a series of letters which you will receive from me, your birth Mother, to let you know that my love for you grows as you grow. I'm sure that when you become old enough to receive these communications from me, you will know that my love for you has been, as it is now, even stronger. Never ending.

I think of you always, with much love. I believe that Andrea and Scott are very nurturing and loving parents for you. You are the light of many lives. It is my belief that you are strong in your natural spirit, as am I.

Know Seren/Bruce, that you are much loved, and of great importance.

With all my heart-Katherine

~ Serenaid ~

August 6, 1987

Dear Harvey, Andrea, Scott and Bruce/Seren,

Hello to all. I'm attempting to write and communicate simply what is going on with me. I have relocated to a lovely little beach town in the North County of San Diego-Leucadia. I like living here very much. It isn't Spain, but it certainly isn't L.A... Anyway, I found a cozy little seafood café to work in. I get along well with the owners with whom I work and with all the locals and tourists who come for good seafood.

This fall I will continue to go to college, taking Sociology and Spanish. I really would love to do a play or at least take a drama class and I may forfeit the Spanish class for the drama, as time doesn't allow me to do everything at once.

I'm still in a recovery 'mode' as far as giving Bruce/Seren to you for good care. And other significant losses. However, I'm feeling better and better. It's just difficult at certain times. I'm sure you can understand...You must know I feel I have made a wise and loving decision and I love you all...

I'm glad I finally wrote this letter to you. I put if off for quite a while. Andrea, would you mind sending me some pictures of (current) Bruce? I'd sure like that.

I guess that's about it for now-my very best to all of you! And thank you Harvey, for forwarding this letter for me. I hope to hear from you soon.

God Bless You.

Katherine xo

September 1, 1987

Dear Katherine,

It was so good to hear from you and that you sound so happy in your new home. The summer was pretty uneventful here, but we did have lots of company, so I was busy. In June, we got a nineteen year old girl from Sweden to come and live with us and help me with Bruce. They get along great. Once he started crawling and climbing (at 5 months), his screaming, frustrated earlier days ended and he became a new baby. He loves his Gymboree and 'Mommy and Me' groups and is the most active boy wherever we go (and the most beautiful). My girlfriend calls him Mr. Personality.

We couldn't be happier. I'm enclosing some photos—I hope I didn't send any of these before—with approximate dates. I've put your letters in the safety deposit box. Would there be a way to get a photo of you and Anders for the future? Scott, Bruce and I send all our love.

Andrea

September 14, 1987

Dear Andrea,

Thank you so much for your 'Dance' card and letter. A special thanks for the pictures of Bruce, "Mr.

Personality". I have no doubt he is one of life's greats.

I am looking for some pictures of myself and Anders, I don't know if I will find any-but I'll include what I have with this letter. Also, I spoke with Siv, Anders' mother in Sweden, earlier this week and she will try and send some pictures. She was supportive.

I am getting rather busy now with school and work. Enjoy both.

As ever Andrea, I hold you, Bruce and Scott close to my heart.

With love,

Katherine

This letter had been written on the back of a piece of paper in which Katherine Xeroxed a picture of her hand for Bruce to have.

October, 1987

Dear Katherine,

Sorry this has taken a few weeks but I got company right after I spoke with you. Thank you so much for the call, it really means a lot to me. Harvey was here today and now we are all in agreement, Bruce is a real pistol! Eating food, reaching and grabbing and smiling up a storm. The photos are all at about 9 or 10 weeks, nothing as cute as Bruce in the swing has been taken since, but we're working on it. Both of your notes are in the safety deposit box.

Take care of yourself, we all love you,

Bruce, Andrea and Scott

In a holiday card we sent to Katherine a brief note was included...

November, 1987

Dear Katherine,

We want to wish you the best at this holiday season. Thank you so much for the pictures. We are all well here. I had corrective surgery on my hand and it is doing great. Bruce is tall and beautiful and we are happy and we love you.

Andrea

In November, 1987, a letter came from our adoption attorney to file a Petition and Accounting Report with the check request to the Clerk of the Superior Court. It was to be completed and then the filing for our hearing date to finalize our adoption would proceed. By late January, 1988, our hearing had been set for February 12th. We got our video camera ready and took Bruce to the downtown Los Angeles courthouse. On February 23, we a signed an Adoption Decree and awaited our new birth certificate that announced our child will henceforth be named BRUCE ZARON MATIS.

On Bruce's first birthday, the phone rang. I was

wearing my white cotton turtleneck and olive green khaki wool pants. I had long brown hair and was feeling I had the look of a new mom. I usually wore sweatpants and sweatshirts because Brucie dribbled all the time and I didn't want to ruin my good clothes. But this birthday was different. Bruce was having his first birthday party. All of our friends and family came. There was birthday cake in his hair, on the floor, everywhere. We laughed so hard while he tried to put the cake in his mouth that actually ended up all over his hair.

The guests had left. Just my folks were still hanging around when the phone rang. I went to the kitchen.

"Andie? Hi. It's Katherine". I was somewhat dumbfounded. I wasn't sure what to say.

"Hi! How are you?" She told me she was living down near San Diego.

"I wanted to wish Seren a Happy Birthday." She was readjusting to life and taking care of herself. She sounded more serious, but okay with life. I talked quietly, not wanting my parents in the next room to know Bruce's birth mother was on the phone. I felt uncomfortable, but wanted to make sure she was okay and that she knew we were all fine. I told her we had gotten the birthday card she had sent. It was a little awkward for our first conversation in a year and at that moment I just wasn't sure how I felt about the call.

The next day I phoned Harvey to tell him I was feeling a little confused about the setup. So we worked out a definite plan. Pictures were to be sent twice a year through Vista. No phone calls unless arranged through Harvey first. We could always find each other through the agency, but we were not revealing our home address to her just yet. We truly had to see how it all worked out. As time passed and we understood what an exceptional relationship we had with our birth mother, the middle man didn't seem necessary. But at first, with defenses up, we protected our personal space until our communications became deeper and more profound. Harvey contacted Katherine and all was well with the plan. She began sending beautiful letters to Bruce/Seren which she called him for years. We finalized the adoption in court with an attorney when Bruce was 18 months old. More pictures. By then, he had long golden ringlets and was husky and strong. We let Katherine know when he was walking and talking and she kept us up to date on her life in Southern California.

Katherine established a pattern with us early on by sending Bruce a birthday card every year. She also never missed sending me a Mother's Day card, until she had a family of her own. We were slowly becoming sisters of sorts.

January 26, 1988

Dearest Andrea,

Happy, healthy New Year to you, et al!! I <u>*thank*</u> *you for your holiday card. It was perfect timing for me to receive it. I came home from a long trip (car to Sacramento). It was late at night when I got home and it was my* <u>*birthday*</u>*. Your card topped off a wonderful holiday time,*

I wanted to send congratulations and best wishes to Bruce on his first birthday. I called Harvey to relay my *message to you but he suggested I call you myself. I don't know if that would have been wanted OR appropriate. I didn't want to take away any of the glory of that day. But you can be sure my <u>heart</u> was with you all. As it is always. May I have some pictures of Bruce on his first birthday? Family pictures of you and Scott and Bruce warm my heart, as I can be secure in knowing how loved he is with you!*

You mentioned having corrective surgery (on your hands). Wonderful! Tell me about it. How are you feeling? What differences has it made for you?

I'm keeping busy with working and volunteering for the local Red Cross, doing casework. Interesting!

ONLY LOVE FOR ALL

Katherine

Katherine, on the other hand had come a long way to get where she was. During her pregnancy she thought long and hard about what to do. She would close her eyes and imagine her unborn child, Seren, as she had always called him. She wanted to help him in every way possible. He would be in a nice home, with a stable family who would love and care for him. A safe environment. She held this image in her heart as she decided to pick the right parents for him. She recognized her dreams of keeping him as just that, knowing that a succession of menial jobs and coming home to a rented room were not the life she felt Seren deserved. Keeping her baby would be a dream she would have loved, but a reality she could not accept.

After her third meeting with her social worker,

Katherine reviewed the dossiers from three couples. Immediately, she connected with us, especially me. We were the same age and both loved to dance. She appreciated the hard times we had dealt with resulting from my illness and felt the strength it had given our relationship. She felt secure that Seren would be given a dependable family. As she read the profiles, she realized she had lived and worked near a hotdog stand, although she couldn't remember the names of the owners. Harvey, her counselor, told her that Scott had owned the Wiener Factory and she thought to herself, "what a strange coincidence."

When Scott recognized Katherine as Harpo, they both laughed. She reminded people of Harpo Marx, thick, blonde curly hair and very agile and comical. Katherine started humming the tune to 'The Twilight Zone' and the original interview was well underway. The ice breaker had come for us all and the interview became real, serious and completely down to earth.

Katherine was so pleased that we were so concerned about her pregnancy and health. She felt great, was eating well, taking vitamins and getting her rest. She wasn't sure exactly how long she had been pregnant, but gave an estimate. At the end of her last trimester, dripping wet, she was just a solid 118 pounds! She wanted to know about our religion and we told her we were both Jewish and would raise the baby Jewish. Katherine was fine with that and even put Jewish on Bruce/Seren's birth certificate. She constantly amazed us with her strength and love for Seren. She wanted him to have a spiritual home, to be raised with traditions and values. She felt deeply that we could give him that.

During our first interview, I began to tell Katherine

about me. "I had been dancing in a company when I first started to get sick. That was so hard to give up, so I took up painting to keep my hands moving." Katherine acknowledged she had always wanted to be a dancer, but had never made a serious commitment. "But that was why I was attracted to your profile, because you were like my inner dream…a dancer." She too was feeling a special connection to us. We told her all about our home, how much we loved where we lived. How beautiful it was and that we couldn't even believe it was really ours. "It's like Hawaii, Koa wood everywhere, palm trees, stain glass, so warm and so us!"

The house sounded beautiful to Katherine; although it was the one house she never did see. Through all the talking, Katherine had never even noticed my hands. At the end of the interview, as she stood up to say goodbye and leave the office, her eyes were transfixed on my fingers. I froze. She turned to Harvey and casually asked, "Can she pick up the baby?" Harvey put his arms around her and confirmed that we knew we would hire full time help, although I would also be available at all times. Katherine accepted the fact that Seren would be well cared for and never felt concern for his physical safety or welfare. In that way, she was the person we needed. One who could see beyond my disability and into my heart. One of her many special attributes.

When Katherine returned home to her aunt's house after the meeting, her aunt got in her face. "Are you sure you should be meeting them like this? You are going to give them a healthy white baby, you should ask for at least ten thousand dollars. Do you realize what this baby is worth?" Katherine was stunned and appalled, "Eeewwww," she said. "You might not want to be saying these things to me!" This attitude upset and frustrated Katherine greatly.

Her aunt was extremely irritated, but Katherine had made her choice and was sticking to it. In her heart, she felt that she had found Seren's rightful parents and she trusted her own intuition more than what her family had to say. Then, her aunt came back at her, "Why don't you give the baby to me? I've always wanted a child. A lot of relatives adopt their own family's unwanted babies". This sounded very harsh and Katherine knew that it would be a huge mistake to go that route and stuck firm to her decision. Just as Katherine dealt with her family issues, we continued to deal with ours, "You're not going to keep in touch with the mother, are you? What if she wants him back?" The old perception of adoption was still there in the 1980's. These unsupportive comments went by the wayside as both Katherine and I knew that this arrangement was right for both of us. We had no questions in our hearts. The birth announcement read,

> Born in the USA!
> Andrea and Scott Matis
> Are the proud parents of
> Bruce Zaron Matis
> Born January 8, 1987
> 7 lbs., 11.5 ounces, 19 inches

~ Serenaid ~

Chapter Five

Family Album

The Matis Family At The Pool

Acrylic Painting by Andrea Berman Matis

Anders in the seventies.

Anders left, with Katherine and friend.

Andrea at rehearsal.

Andrea in Greece

*Andrea at the 1984 Olympics in
Los Angeles*

Andrea and Scott's Wedding Photo.

Andrea, Scott and Bruce
In New York, 1987

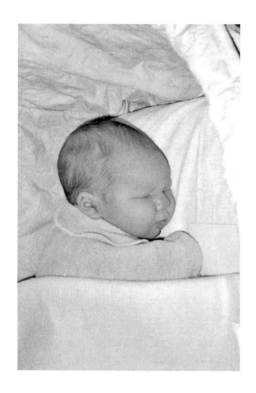

Bruce Newborn

Bruce Age One

Bruce in a Tuxedo Age Two

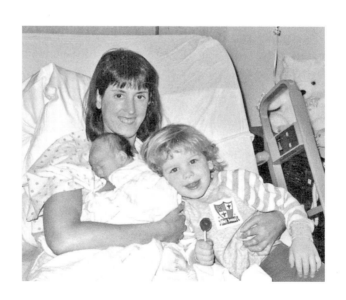

Andrea, Bruce and newborn Blaine

to be a child
is to know the
fun of living
to have a child
is to know the
beauty of life

Blaine's Birth Announcement

Bruce and Blaine, 1990

Bruce, Blaine and Brooke, 1991

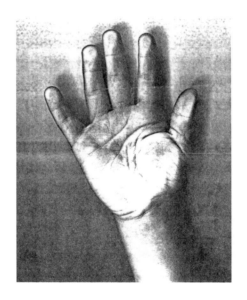

Bruce's Hand sent to Katherine

Our Family: Andrea Berman Matis

For their eighth wedding anniversary, Andrea and Scott Matis of Agoura celebrated their most special "gift" yet — the birth of their daughter Blaine Esty on November 14!

For Andrea, the road to motherhood had been rocky. In 1983, she was diagnosed with scleroderma, a rheumatic disease of the connective tissue, which can affect joints, muscles and internal organs. "I suddenly found that I couldn't even touch my toes," says the former dancer and dance instructor, "and the ulcerations on my fingers wouldn't heal."

After one year of tests she was finally diagnosed with scleroderma. For the first two years Andrea was hospitalized so often that she had to quit working and dancing. During this time she took heavy, experimental medications.

"... a perfect way to blend my dance background and personal experience... with arthritis."

Because the possible effects of the disease on her kidneys were unknown, she was advised by a rheumatologist to wait five years before trying to bear children. As she and Scott wanted to start a family sooner, they decided to adopt. And so Bruce entered their lives, barely one day old!

Except for a few brief periods, Andrea has been off heavy medications for four years. Her pregnancy and delivery were fairly normal, and only in her sixth month did scleroderma symptoms become a problem. She began to have spasms in her esophagus, which were so painful she couldn't sit up or eat, and she began to lose weight.

After one day of testing, the doctors learned that two drugs, Reglan and Tagamet, could control the spasms and pain without harming the baby. The result of Andrea and her doctors' conscientious efforts were more than rewarded with the birth of beautiful, healthy Blaine Esty!

In a few months, Andrea hopes to resume teaching "Joint Efforts," "PACE" and the Arthritis Self-Help Course. "Teaching these classes is a perfect way to blend my dance background and personal experiences of coping with arthritis," she says. Andrea certainly should know — she's come a long way in these past six years.

Congratulations to the Matis family, and welcome Blaine Esty!

> For more information about scleroderma and the Foundation's scleroderma support group, call the Chapter at 213/938-6111.

A happy family—Scott, Bruce and Andrea are still celebrating the arrival of Blaine Esty, born in November.

> The Orange County Branch acknowledges with thanks a bequest of $54,484 from the estate of Frederick Appleby, who often contributed to the Branch during his life and also remembered the Arthritis Foundation in his will.

"Arthritis in Prime Time" Coming for Young Adults

"Arthritis in Prime Time," a two-day symposium for young adults with arthritis and those who care about them, will be held Saturday and Sunday, September 15 and 16 in Los Angeles.

Actress Victoria Principal, who has been a national spokesperson for the Arthritis Foundation for many years, will be a keynote speaker at a luncheon in her honor to be held during the Sunday session.

The general sessions and workshops are designed to help people with arthritis, family members, friends, and health professionals better understand the medical and lifestyle issues which arthritis presents in the prime of life and to learn new ways to cope with them.

Due to the past success of the first two seminars which began in 1986, "Arthritis in Prime Time" has expanded to two days and is being offered nationwide.

Registration brochures with more details will be available in mid-February. The registration fee will be $40 per person for the two days, or $35 per person for family groups of more than one.

Call your local branch or the Chapter office at (213) 938-6111 for a brochure in February, but save the date now.

Warner Center News

Andrea Matis and son Bruce of Woodland Hills enjoy a quiet moment reading together. Andrea, who has a form of arthritis called scleroderma, is one of five mothers the Arthritis Foundation's Southern California chapter is saluting in honor of Mother's Day and in recognition of May as national Arthritis Month.

Andrea continues to lead an active life with the help of the Chapter. She works in the San Fernando Valley as an Arthritis Foundation exercise instructor for "Joint Efforts", a class that helps people with arthritis maintain joint mobility, and as an arthritis self-help course leader.

Newspaper Article

Andrea's Drawing of her Father

Matis Family Photo, 1992

The Evolution of Fatherhood by Bruce

Please share in our happiness
as our son

Bruce

is called to the Torah
as a Bar Mitzvah
Saturday, the eighth of January
in the year two thousand
at nine-thirty in the morning
Temple Beth Haverim
5126 Clareton Drive
Agoura Hills, California

Luncheon reception immediately following
Duke's Malibu

Andrea and Scott Matis

Bruce's Bar Mitzvah Invitation, 2000

Katherine and Mark's Wedding

Katherine and Chelsea

The Families Together in Maui, 2002

Chapter Six

A Family Formed

We took our new baby home while Katherine dreamt of him. We held him in our arms while Katherine longed for him. We were ecstatic; she was filled with grief. She cried daily and we simply could not wipe the smiles off our faces. She mourned in isolation, telling only Harvey, her social worker, her day to day feelings. She longed to hear from us and prayed her son was safe and secure. Our contact kept her going. Each letter she received from us helped her let go just a little bit more. She started to hold her breath less and knew that this was best for Seren. Knowing that he was in loving hands and keeping her in the loop helped her survive that first year. As the pictures came, the pain began to lessen and as time passed the communications opened more and more and a loving and supportive extended family began to form for all of us.

Bruce began to grow through all of those wonderful baby stages. He started by rolling over and of course, we were amazed. Soon he sat up. I was sure no other child had ever done that before. Then he started crawling and before we knew it, he was 'cruising' the furniture and I was finding out about walking shoes. Magic Johnson and Chick Hearn from the Lakers would have said he was 'motating'. He stepped and stepped and finally at thirteen months, he was off and running. And all the while he babbled. Yakity Yak. It was constant. He had this sweet high sing song kind of voice and we never tired of listening to it. By the time we took him on our first holiday to the Hawaiian Islands at fifteen months, Bruce had over seventy five words in his baby vocabulary, seventy five percent of which even people who weren't his parents or friends could understand. Some words were indeed in a language all his own. Adidi was an airplane. Cakananni meant anything that was crunchy, like Cheerios or crackers. Then the singing began. At Gymboree, he joined in with all the mommies and by My Gym he knew all the words to "Wheels on the Bus". He delighted us with his beautiful voice and love for music and comedy. How many times did he tell me the joke about 'I told the doctor it hurts when I do this' and the doctor said 'Don't do that!" In his tuxedo he would stand by his bedroom door while Scott's sister, Aunt Gale and I videotaped his many one-liners, "Take my mom, please!" He continued to quote all the characters from Sesame Street, especially Oscar the Grouch and Cookie Monster. Bruce would hide in our pantry trash can thinking he was Oscar. He would even disappear at the park and give us such a fright until we took a second to think and then go find him in the park trash can. "Look mommy, I'm Oscar the grouch!" he would say.

In September of 1987, it was time. I made an appointment with Dr. Meals at UCLA to discuss hand surgery. I had waited my five years, I was stable and strong. He agreed. I was put under 'twilight' and when I came to, my hand had been re-set into a much more functional position. Four of my fingers were cleaned from bad bone and then broken and rewired back together. I could hold things better, including Bruce. It looked way better, but that was relative. I continued to shake hands with my left hand so that no one would touch my new metal wiring. I was paranoid about the metal detector at the airport, but I did not make the buzzer go off the first time I went though. I had a new hand. The miracles of modern medicine continued to astound me.

February, 1988

Dear Katherine,

Hello! How are you? We are all doing fine. As you can tell from his photo, Bruce is really something else. He doesn't crawl any more and his vocabulary is about 8 or 9 words. My hands are feeling fine and I have started back to art class. Scott is busy with hot dogs-still! We're trying to plan a Trip to Hawaii in the later spring for the family. Bruce's first birthday was a thrill and we think of you often.

All our love,

Andrea, Scott and Bruce

April 14, 1988

Dear Katherine,

We just wanted to drop you a note to keep in touch- so, how are you? I hope all is treating you well. We're all fine here. I have been doing some etchings in my art class and teaching programs for the Arthritis Foundation. Scott is busy with selling Christmas Trees and Bruce doesn't shut up, although we don't know what he's saying half the time. Scott and I have just completed an "Adoption Workshop" sponsored by Vista Del Mar where we really learned a lot of good things. Most of all, we learned what a good adoption process we have been through. One of the things we learned was to keep communication lines open at all times. If phone calls are important, they are fine with us. If there's any more things you want Bruce to have (the Tree from Sweden?) please send them. If there is still a possibility of getting any more info or photos from Anders, Bruce would appreciate that some day, too. Not to compare—but of all the couples we met at the workshop and all the stories we heard, OURS is the most special of all. We love you very much and if there is anything you ever need—we are always here for you whenever you want!! Keep in touch.

Love,

Andrea and Scott

April 19, 1988

Dearest Andrea,

Boy! You know how to make a girl feel good! Thank you so very much for your insightful letter-definition-n. 1-the ability to see and understand clearly the inner nature of things, especially by intuition. 2- an instance of such understanding-AND for those beautiful pictures! I cried with such joy! How God has touched our lives is wonderful. Bruce is so loved by many.

I tried calling Anders at work (in Madrid), but he wasn't in, so I left my number for him to return my call. I want to let him know of the importance of keeping in touch. And pretty much just further communication, like what you

112

said in your letter. So, we'll see.

Love living here! I'm still working at the restaurant and volunteering with the Red Cross. I'm taking Jazz Technique and Jazz. Love dancing again. Feeling better, thinking of you all and grateful to have you in Bruce's and my life...

I'm sending a Swedish 'Midsummer Tree" for Bruce. It is a special token of love in my life, given to me from Anders. I now pass it on to B.Z. The Swedes love summer—love the sun, because the country is usually so cold, dark and blanketed with snow much of the time. When spring and summer arrive, theirs is a most glorious sight. Beautiful flowers and greenery everywhere. To celebrate, the people make Mid Summer Trees made from green leafy branches and fresh picked flowers. The actual trees may be taller than a house. I guess it's something like our Maypoles.

The seminar you and Scott attended sounds very positive. I agree totally—communication is the approach to take for nurturing lives and relationships.

Again Andrea, Scott and dear Bruce—I love you all very much. XXOO

Yours,

Katherine

May, 1988

Dear Katherine,

Thanks so much for the gift for Bruce. I think he

speaks way over 40 words now. We took him to Hawaii, so here are some new pix. All here is very well. Take care!

Love,

Andrea, Scott and Bruce

P.S. Check out this very special news paper clipping!

A month later, I received my first Mother's Day card from Katherine. The front of the card read: *A Mother's Day Wish for You.*

The inside read: *"Mother's Day is a time when we think of those who mean so very much." Because you mean so very much, this comes to wish you a Mother's Day filled with all the beauty a day can bring, all the love a heart can hold...all the happiness you so deserve. HAPPY MOTHER'S DAY."* And to that she added, *"Thinking of you on this Special Day".*

> *With Love in My Heart,*
> *Katherine.*

At night when he was getting older Bruce would wake up, climb out of his crib and sneak into our bedroom. Quietly he would whisper in my ear 'Soy milk' and I would get him a bottle to drink that was safe for his many ear infections. Then we would go back to the rocking chair in his room and sing 'Jet Plane' together until he dozed off again on my shoulder. There was many a night that I sang that song to Bruce to fall asleep by. And there was a good reason.

114

When I was younger and even into my adulthood, I had a wonderful friend named Chuck. He and his brother were identical twins at my summer sleep away camp in Bucks County, Pennsylvania. He was a folk singer and a mentor to me when I got to college and he lived nearby my new home when I moved to Southern California, in 1972. He taught me about telling the truth no matter what the cost and I will never forget him for that. It had such an impression on me from high school on. After I was married and started to become ill, I went to Philly to see Chuck. He had moved back there from Los Angeles and we had a good laugh together.

I was just starting to feel less energetic and longing for old friends and the warmth they brought me. A few months after we returned home, my sister told me that Chuck had a brain tumor. I couldn't believe my ears. I had just read, *When Bad Things Happen to Good People*. Reality hit hard and more often as I got older. One night when I was on that magical vacation with cousins Sheri and Brian to St. John, I had this awful feeling overcome me while listening to my cousin play guitar and sing during a Caribbean sunset. When I returned to LA, I found out that Chuck had passed away that same evening. It was the first time that I knew someone who was sick and died besides a family member and I was heartsick. After that, I would have these strange experiences. I would be lying in bed and I would feel a presence in the room. Chuck would advise me or give me spiritual or political commentary. I could feel him, even see him in the room on several occasions and it was very overpowering. One time the apparition was so strong that I even contacted his brother, as strange as I felt in doing so, and told him that Chuck had been with me and that he was good!

After Bruce was born, I never had that feeling again. I knew that my good friend had come back to me through Bruce. We took Bruce back east to Philadelphia and had dinner at my friend Jaime's house in Elkins Park, Pennsylvania. Chuck's brother, Hank, came to meet Bruce and somehow we all had closure. Chuck's favorite song had been "Jet Plane." So was his twin brother Hank's.

August 15, 1988

Dearest Andrea, Scott and Baby Bruce,

Hi! I just wanted to let you in on the latest with me and to keep in touch as always. I wish I had some current pictures to send-but I don't. I imagine there will be some coming next Holiday Time. There are a lot of changes in the making with me and my life. My "boyfriend" Stephen and I have been in counseling for a month together. Stephen has a severe problem with depression and brings it to our coupling relationship. Not an easy trick for me to handle. I'm looking into trying to find a roommate situation with a girlfriend. In other words, time to go.

It's scary, the money isn't there. I make so little of it at this time. But I'm determined to have good things in my life, and that I will do.

I've just registered for two college classes in the fall. I'm taking Psychology and Acting. I'm involved with this Theatre group and will try to make time to be in their Christmas program, "A Christmas Carol," the Dickens version.

I'm still holding my own at the café and looking for

another p/t situation for making $$. Without a car or bike, life moves at a mysterious pace ...SLOW, with a lot of effort!

Any words from Anders yet?

Only love for all,

Katherine
A special kiss and hug for XO Bruce XO

Bruce began to serenade us repeatedly. His song repertoire grew as did our ability to listen to him sing for hours. Twinkle Twinkle, ABC's, and Old MacDonald. His voice was so sweet and he always had perfect pitch. I would write letters to Katherine telling her that Bruce would never shut up or stop singing. She loved hearing it. One day we were at a second birthday party for a little friend of Bruce's down the street in Woodland Hills, Noah. He started to play with a new little boy and we began to talk to his parents. Their son's name was Connor. We loved that name. We had even thought about it for Bruce because we had seen the movie, "The Terminator" with my friend Cindy and the lead character's name was Sarah Connor. She was such a strong willed character, the name rang true. We thought that was a great name for a boy, but we had to go with Bruce. Years later, when Bruce was in middle school, he came home talking about this kid who played awesome guitar in a band at school. His new friend Connor was actually his old acquaintance from years ago. It's a small world after all! Later, they would form a garage band, Scarlet Rose, that moved into the studio and performed at clubs like the legendary 'Whiskey A Go Go' on Sunset Boulevard in Hollywood! Scarlet Rose was long in the making.

September 6, 1988

Dear Katherine,

Just a little note to update you on Bruce. And a couple of photos too. Bruce is a verbal machine—about 100 words! Several in Spanish (casa) but even more fun, he knows about 8 in sign language—my sister teaches him to sign when they play. He <u>loves</u> to dance. He's a real whirling dervish and he loves Sesame Street too.

I've been taking painting classes and working for the Arthritis Foundation and Scott's busy selling Christmas Trees, peaches and apples. We're also busy fixing up the house.

We took Bruce to see his great-grandmother, my MomMom in Baltimore and they were best friends. It was wonderful...

I'm reading a great book, *A Woman of Independent Means*, I think you'd like it. I like all her books, Elizabeth F. Hailey.

So, how are you? What are you doing? We think of you often and hope you are well. If the gypsy in you takes you out of California-make sure we know where!

All our love, and good wishes-

Andrea, Scott and Bruce

November 30, 1988

~ Serenaid ~

Dearest Bruce, Andrea and Scott,

Just a short note to let you know I think of you often and especially at Holiday time. I'm at the end of my college semester and have done well so far (it's a mystery to me!) and now it's finals and term papers. It can be intimidating if you've been out of school as long as I have!

Please find enclosed a bird from Bali, a Star of David from Mexico and a newspaper clipping of my work mates and I hamming it up for the local press. The bird and star are for Bruce with all my love. I trust you all will have a wonderful Holiday Season.

Lovingly yours,

Katherine

December, 1988

Dear Katherine,

I hope this holiday season finds you in good health and happiness. Last time I got a letter from you, I'm confident you received one from me on the very same day and that we were on the same writing wavelength. I have been fine and even sold my first (really second) painting and maybe another one this week. Scott's busy at work, possibly going for a new career move….Bruce doesn't shut up---and we understand most of what he says now. He's been a real doll (most of the time). We wish you the best for the holidays and the New Year to come.

All our love,

Bruce, Andrea and Scott

One night in late 1988, Scott and I were driving on the Ventura Freeway heading to the 405 South interchange. Bruce was almost two. I had been thinking how lucky I had been. How this little boy brought life back to me. My life had been so discouraging and menacing and then he came along and made it wonderfully worthwhile. I was thinking that it would be so nice for him to have a sibling. I had been thinking about it for some time, but dared not jinx the wonderful life I was leading. I looked left, over to Scott as we drove down the ramp and as I started to speak, Scott looked to his right at me and AT THE VERY SAME TIME we both said, "Do you think we could get another baby?" Then we both said, "What did you say?" And we were cracking up. We decided to talk to my rheumatologist, Lilly to see what she had to say about my abilities to raise a second child with my current health situation. Later we called Lilly and her husband Fred and made a sushi dinner date to talk.

Lilly was so happy to hear how well everything was going with my health and the raising of Bruce. I had been seeing more of Dr. Galpin now and traveled less to Lilly's office in Beverly Hills. So, we asked her, "Do you think we should adopt again?" And she looked at us and took one long deep breath and said, "Well, you did conceive. Just because you didn't take the pregnancy full term, doesn't mean you won't the second time around. About one in four first pregnancies end in miscarriages".

"What are you saying?" And Lilly told us to go back to Dr. Adler and try artificial inseminations again.

She said she and Fred were ready to start their family as well and how wonderful it would be for us to get pregnant together. I said "Really??" and she said "Yes, go for it." And once again I made that phone call asking if I could do insemination on Medicare. Dr. Adler called me back and told me he would never not take me back as a patient due to cost and that he would accept my current health plan. And so, once AGAIN, Scott was off to the races, so to speak!!

In January, 1989, Bruce's second birthday card arrived from Katherine, with an "I love you dear" signature. Always so heartfelt and real. In February, our next letter came.

February 2, 1989

My Dearest Andrea,

HI! I trust this letter finds you happy, healthy and loving life! I really just want to make contact with you and propose a kind of plan or schedule—if you will—for communication. And to send my love!

Here's what's happening with me…sometimes I worry (needlessly, I'm sure) when I haven't heard from you in, shall I say, a longer period of time than I expected. Currently, or recently, I'm referring to Bruce's second birthday update and a picture. I want to pause here and interject my feelings on the delicacy of this matter. I always put myself (try to) in your shoes and try to see how you might feel and react to communications with me, like sending me photos—letters—notes. Like you don't have enough to do already? I find it difficult to keep up with all of the letter writing, picture sending, and updating to my family and friends. There is also the possible issue of you perhaps feeling that this is too much communication too often. Well. I'm open to that also. All I want, bottom line here Andrea, is for Bruce, you and Scott to have a fully functioning and loving family life. I want the best for you individually and collectively.

Andrea, I'm not the most eloquent writer or speaker on the planet. I hope I don't leave room for misunderstanding. As I am beginning this letter, I am stuck trying to say everything just so, as to not offend or be unclear, not too mushy, not too blunt...geez...

Can we, together, agree on certain times of the year where we will communicate and send pictures? I'm thinking this will alleviate my wondering and worrying, as well as lessen your burden of, "Well, I should write to Katherine". Tell me what YOU think. I'm thinking two times a year (although if you WANT to write more often...it's always wonderfully received by me!) Perhaps a Holiday and a birthday picture and a mid-summer exchange. If at any time you feel this is not in the best interest of all or any one person—I'm always open to your needs.

Finally, Andrea, I hope that by giving definition to our communication schedule, all will be well served.

All My Love and Warm Wishes,

Katherine

P.S. Did you happen to see the Brazilian Dance Troupe, "OBA-OBA" when they were in L.A.? Girl, I'm talking HOT!

In January, I headed back to Beverly Hills, first with a full and painful bladder and also with a small specimen jar of semen between my legs. I remember watching David Steinberg, the comedian on TV, tell his story about fertility. He was describing the fertility clinic he and his wife went to. There was no doubt that Victor was his lab technician and they had gone through what I had gone through and what I was about to go through again, at the same doctor's office. I was ready for my first artificial insemination since my miscarriage. Two weeks later, my period arrived, un-welcomed. Then two weeks later, I was back on the Ventura Freeway doing that oh so familiar drive. I had even been to an acupuncturist for some back pain from an earlier car accident and asked him to go ahead and hit those fertility spots while he was at it. My health was good, I was not on any meds and I was mentally strong. But only to a certain point. I gave myself six months this time around, instead of the ten it took last time. Then, if nothing worked, we would head back to Vista Del Mar and start all over again, or even better yet, to one of the few lawyers I had read about or that friends had used and recommended to start the adoption process all over again. Now that we were educated, I felt I could go to an attorney for an adoption.

March 4, 1989

Dear Katherine,

Needless to say, it's been a hectic two months since New Year's. I am enclosing the only picture I have of Bruce right now and I'm confident I've already sent you one since this one is months old already. As soon as I get it together, I will send copies of a much more recent photo. Nothing from his birthday party came out great and something happened to the camera on our latest roll of film and so it was exposed, snow pictures and all.

Your schedule sounds great, and as you know, in the past, I have tried my best to be a good letter writer and photo sender. But these past few months have been monstrous, so I'll give you a little update and then promise to be my best on all communications in the future.

At Christmas time, my grandmother, in Baltimore, had some heart problems (continuing from years before) and my mother left L.A. on New Year's Day as my grandmother, MomMom (my mom's mom) was going to have open heart surgery in early January. She did (she is 87 years old) and is slowly recovering and my Mom returned this week. So, in February, when my babysitter quit, I was working three days a week, shuffling Bruce around between my dad and friends (and even strange babysitters a few times - ugh) and basically getting a good feel for the working Mom without good childcare. It was a month-long process replacing her with a lovely woman from Guatemala and I am feeling much more settled and rested now. Then, in early January, a friend of mine from work at the Arthritis Foundations was killed in a tragic accident. I literally could not think for about three weeks. I was spaced-out like never before, forgetful, oblivious, you name it. Then, I was called and offered her job! So, I am now the Secretary for the Arthritis Foundation!

So, needless to say, I have been busy and things are just starting to settle down. Scott went away skiing last week and we are now planning for a summer vacation (Europe? London, I hope). Bruce must be taking after

Anders as he can already count to ten in English and Spanish. He almost knows the whole alphabet too. And, as you know, he is still, Mr. Personality. He just blows me away. He is tall (36") but slim (28 lbs.). He never shuts up, singing and talking all the time.

So, I'm sorry if you feel any delay in our communications, but I will do my best from now on. We think of you often and we wonder things like: Does Katherine have a really loud voice? Does she bend her knees when she runs? Will she only take bubble baths? How curly was her hair when she was little? Does she have big feet?

Anyway, you can guess how much we think of you and hope all is well and wonderful in your end of California. I must close with a short but incredible story—we met friends who also adopted a boy in 1987 through Vista, at the workshop we took last year. In January, they were called by Vista with news of another baby-a girl, that was born to the same birthmother as their first child and that she was available for adoption. Needless to say, they adopted Adam's half sister and are now indeed the ultimate nuclear family. It was such a heartwarming story, that Scott and I (hush, not even my Mom or anyone knows) are now considering our next steps for a sibling for Bruce. We'll probably let Harvey know our intentions by late summer when Bruce heads off to preschool. I don't know how Vista works the second time around, so we have a lot of checking out to do (attorneys too, etc.).

Anyway, Bruce loves other kids and babies. My girlfriend has triplets and he has a blast at her house.

Old Blue Eyes couldn't be any cuter if he tried and so in all happiness, health and thoughtfulness—I sign off, promising to send a two year photo ASAP.

All our love and warm wishes,
Andrea, Scott and Bruce Z

I drove back to the Los Angeles Fertility clinic in mid March. Dr. Danzer was on call this time. After my insemination, I stayed on the table with my hips up and my body very still. Things felt right. After twenty minutes, I got up and got dressed and went home. The next ten days seemed like an eternity. On day thirty-one of my cycle, I had NOT gotten a period. I was getting a little excited. Just a little. The doctor told me to come in for a urine and blood test. Again, I faced the 101 and sped to the other side of the hill. I was called in for my tests. In only a few short minutes, the urine test was positive. I was pregnant! It seems that Scott's 100,000,000 sperm count worked and I made a hand painted T-shirt with little sperm dots all over it that read, "One Hundred Million and counting!" I don't think I took a breath the whole drive home, and on the doctor's advice, I had a bottle of champagne waiting on the Koa wood bar when Scott arrived. We decided NOT to tell anyone until the completion of my first trimester because it was so difficult to have to explain my miscarriage to people the last time around. People I hadn't seen in a while after I had told them I was pregnant thought that I had delivered Bruce when they got my birth announcement. I didn't want to explain that type of situation ever again. It was very distressing and emotional for me.

Unfortunately, I needed an obstetrician as the fertility specialists did not deliver babies. So I did my research, talked to Dr. Galpin and began interviewing doctors that handled high risk pregnancies. We met with three doctors who came highly recommended. All three delivered out of Tarzana Medical, which had a high risk maternity unit, and was about ten minutes from our home. We knew that Cedars Sinai had a great high risk department as well, but it was too far away. We chose Dr. Peter Rubinstein on Etiwanda Street in Tarzana. He was direct, yet warm like a big cuddly teddy bear. He said, "If I can get you to twenty-eight weeks, then that would be great". Dr. Rubinstein knew very little about scleroderma and pregnancy, but he did know that premature deliveries were very likely. He also promised to his best ability, that he would avoid a Caesarian Section at all costs, not wanting to cut me or to have healing complications with my poor circulation. And then my next Mother's Day card arrived, what timing Katherine had! "This is to send you a very special Mother's Day Wish xoxo, From ME to You, Lovingly, Katherine."

June 27, 1989

Dear Katherine,

So much has happened, in the past few months, I really don't know where to begin. All but my grandmother's passing is wonderful news. Let's see: due to neighborhood construction and Scott's job moving to Oxnard, we sold our house and just opened Escrow on a new one, further west. It's 500 square feet bigger and brand new. We should be moved in about five weeks. I fired my housekeeper about two weeks before my work (just one day a week now) ended and my Mom helped me out. Curious how Bruce is a much better boy without her around. We are the best of pals and he is an absolute hit everywhere we go. We've been in a "Mommy and Me" program all year and next week he starts camp all on his own.

Scott's parents will be married 50 years on July third and are having a big wedding celebration in Las Vegas. Guess who the ring bearer will be-wearing a tux and all!!

And now for the most wonderful news of all…the best for last…after a few years of real stabilization of my Scleroderma, Scott and I decided it would be fantastic for Bruce to have a sibling. After confirming with my rheumatologist, I went to a fertility specialist in Beverly Hills…and I am five months pregnant!!! I can't tell you how overwhelmed with happiness we are. Bruce points to my stomach and says, "Baby's heart" and gives it a kiss!

So, as you can see, it's been a busy few months, but all news is good news.

All of our very best love to you—

Andrea, Scott and Bruce

As I taught my Arthritis Exercise Programs to senior citizens, I did my best to keep to a high risk pregnancy physical activity minimum. I was very careful not to overdo activities. I felt pretty good and began to gain some weight. Starting at 98 pounds, I had a ways to go. At the eleven week mark, Dr. Szydlo had me do a new prenatal test. It was called the CVS (Chorionic Villi Sampling). In the first Trimester, they took some embryonic cells to check for genetic diagnostic information so that if there was a problem, it could be attended to early.

In an amniocentesis, you have to be further along in pregnancy. We specifically requested a "DO NOT TELL" on the folder for the sex of the baby. It was stamped all over the folder. With all the planning we had been through in our recent lives, we looked forward to at least one surprise. When the results came back and everything was fine, it was difficult not to ask if it was a boy or a girl, but we held tight. It just didn't matter to us either way.

The inquisition had begun. Scott's mother couldn't bare the thought that the doctor knew the sex of her grandchild and she did not. She kept asking us what it was and we kept telling her that we didn't know. She said, "Of course you know, you're just not telling." We would tell her again that indeed we did not know and we were not asking. Several months went by and Scott's parents were having their 50th wedding anniversary party. They were renewing their wedding vows that no one saw them take years ago when they eloped. They lived in Las Vegas and we were all heading there for the July 4th weekend to celebrate. Bruce was going to be the ring bearer in his tiny tuxedo and walk down the isle with his little cousin, our niece, Emily, the flower girl. Time was going by quickly when I realized I did not have a wedding gift for the happy couple. Scott had no idea what to get them and I sure didn't.

Then I was struck with a brilliant idea. I called the doctor's office in Beverly Hills that had done the CVS procedure. I asked the nurse if I gave her my credit card information, would she please send a Western Union telegram to the Sahara Hotel which would say,

Dear Grandma and Papa,

Happy Fiftieth Anniversary. You are now the first to know I am going to have a baby 'BLANK'.
Love,
Your Grandson

Bruce

I said to the nurse, "PLEASE don't finish the sentence, I don't want to know what it is. Here is the Western Union information. Please call them with my credit card and send the telegram. I will let Grandma tell me what I am having as her gift." The nurse was shocked. "What a great idea and magnificent gift," she told me. "Of course I will call." But it was the July 4th holiday weekend and things didn't go as smoothly as I had wished. The wedding celebration came and went and when Sunday morning arrived, still no telegram from Western Union.

I asked Scott to walk over to the Registration desk again and ask if the telegram had arrived. Finally after breakfast, it was there. We told Grandma to go get her gift. There was a telegram at the front desk in the lobby. "What does it say?" She asked.

"We don't know", we told her.

"What's in it? Tell me!"

"But we honestly don't know!" After a few rounds of debate, Grandma and Papa were headed to the lobby. They had already invited the immediate family up to their suite before we headed back to our perspective hometowns after the wedding weekend. I asked her to bring the telegram up to her room and when she wanted to, to read it silently to herself. Then if she chose, she could read it to her entire family. Everyone kept asking us what it said and we told everyone that we would find out as soon as

Grandma told us!

Scott and I waited with immense anticipation as we all gathered together for Grandma's special gift. And then she opened the envelope and started to read the telegram out loud. Scott said, "No Mom! Read it to yourself first so only you know what it says. Then you can read it out loud." Within seconds, Grandma was crying. She could barely contain herself when she filled in the blanks......proud big brother of a baby sister. And that was when we found out that Bruce was going to have a baby sister and Grandma said, "The perfect family, a boy and a girl." I was to have one of each.

During my second trimester, things began to change at our homestead. I had some problems with my digestion and had to take care of some medical issues. Then, the house we loved so much with its beautiful hillside view, ala the TV show 'Bonanza,' was being invaded. The land above us had been purchased and was being developed. There were sixty-foot posts behind our home marking property lines and cliffhanger homes. One day I looked out the back window and gasped. I picked up the phone and called Scott at the Weiner Factory. "We have to move. You won't believe what I am looking at." When Scott got home from the Weiner Factory and saw the hillside, he said "After all the fixing up we've done, I can't believe this." We put our house on the market and starting looking for new homes in the Conejo Valley. On August first 1989, we moved to Oak Park, where we lived and raised our family for the next fifteen years.

And then, on November 14, 1989, Blaine Esty was born. We had become the All-American nuclear family.

131

~ Serenaid ~

Chapter Seven

Katherine

Across the country from where I grew up in Wilmington, Delaware, another young girl was struggling in Southern California. My home was stable and secure. My parents fell in love after the war and were married during tough times. They lived over the grocery store where my grandparents worked. My older brother Joel was born at '4th and Pine' as they said. But, when I was on the way, my parents left my MomMom's apartment along with my mom's sister, my Aunt Ida, and purchased their first homes across the back alley way from each other on 39th and 40th streets. The two sisters lived back to back for fourteen years with the helpful support of each other and MomMom coming every Saturday morning to make us homemade hot cereal and tea. My dad had a good job in Philadelphia working for the Atlantic Oil Company. The baby boom had arrived.

On the California/Arizona border there was a young woman named Marsha. When she was eighteen years old, she had a baby girl named Katherine and a short lived marriage. She held on as long as she could having been from the Oklahoma Depression era and knowing the importance of having a family income. Marsha was from a family of eight children with an alcoholic father. She had been abused by her older brother at age five. As much as it pains Katherine to admit it, her desires to overcome poverty and excel in her life, did not change her opinion of her self, when in her own words she actually said that a direct descendent of 'white trash'.

133

Katherine's relationship with her mother grew to be sporadic at best. It came and went, but was never what she idealized it would be. They were never close, never like girlfriends and so often Katherine felt abandonment and betrayal. Her dad had disappeared when she was around three and she lost contact with him for years. He had apparently been quite abusive to her mother and she believes most likely to her. Later, when Katherine had the opportunity to meet her biological half-siblings from her father, they confessed to being severely abused by him. Katherine summed him up with one simple phrase. "He was not a nice man!"

Katherine's childhood was a jigsaw puzzle of broken relationships and homes with episodes of abuse and neglect. There were few happy moments. By the time she was five, her mother had another boyfriend who abused Katherine. She remembers her mother picking up and taking her to Kansas to her aunt's house. Her mother had become pregnant by this man, whom she was not married to, and then they split up. Years later, in anger and disgust, Marsha told Katherine that she gave up this man and this child for her. The child had been placed for adoption and Katherine had felt great guilt. After her mother's recuperation from her adoption ordeal in Kansas, she and Katherine returned to the San Fernando Valley in California. Marsha worked full time while Katherine fended for herself, always alone.

All in all, Marsha would marry eight times. Men would buy the beautiful woman new homes that she would fix up and decorate, spending their money until they ran out. She was extremely materialistic. When the 'husband of the day' could no longer provide for her, she would take up with another man.

When Katherine was seven, her mother married Francis, who was a strict disciplinarian. But this time, Katherine thoughts wondered, "Who the hell are you?" She didn't actually say that, but in her mind was thinking, "Oh God, now what? Here we go." He was strict and militaristic and Katherine remembers that she could not answer him without saying, "Yes Sir."

Marsha and Francis had a son, a half brother to Katherine, her only sibling. Ironically, after they were divorced, years later, they remarried. Katherine had even taken on Francis' last name as she felt he truly was the closet thing to a father she ever had. Francis's mother, Katherine's step-grandmother, Nancy, was a positive influence on her life. She was the warmth in her youth that she longed for. Nancy was one of her favorite people on earth, and she truly loved her.   She was kind and married to a wonderful man. They had the marriage that Katherine was searching for. They were enamored with each other. They had Christmas and Thanksgiving at their house. There was always plenty of food on the table and gifts under the tree. They even took Katherine to church: a beautiful Catholic Church where she got to dress in her frilly Sunday best and learned to put money in the donation plate, not dip in and take it! Katherine felt a real family relationship with these people and their reprise or retreat from her disturbed life. She felt like she learned some healthy survival skills from them. That life could indeed be good.

By the time Katherine had reached sixth grade, Marsha and Francis were divorced and Nancy was out of the picture.   Katherine's brother was a baby and they moved frequently from place to place, eventually landing in Arizona. Katherine felt set apart from her new friends and neighbors as she entered Junior High. Her mother got a job working for the Sears Catalog and they lived in a small rental house with little money. However, Marsha soon met Jack, a handsome retired police officer who managed a five and dime store. He made a decent living and was nice to Katherine. But there was always a new dad, a new religion, and many adjustments to be made. Katherine battled with living a life of inconsistency. Her half brother, Tim, went to live with his father. Marsha and Jack managed to stay married for about three years until things once again fell apart for her. Their mutual vanity took a toll on the relationship and then Francis came back into the picture.

Katherine left her first crush on a boy and headed back to the California and soon to a new school in Simi Valley. Although the house was beautiful, Katherine felt she had few clothes and sometimes very little food. While I was making a move from Delaware to New Jersey, leaving cheerleading and dance lessons, Katherine was struggling to find her teenage place in California. A time of growth and transition was upon us both. We were both making new friends and trying to establish ourselves in a more adult world.

Katherine met a young woman named Jaden, who had a profound impact on her life. She turned Katherine on to dance and theatre and the arts and taught her to learn not merely to survive, but to experience life with passion. She took Katherine skinny dipping in waterfalls and showed her poetry and music. They became mutual admirers and Jaden was a good influence on Katherine to keep up her school grades and artistic ambitions. Jaden encouraged Katherine to go to San Diego with her and audition for the San Diego School of Performing Arts. Katherine was even invited back for a second audition. But her mother's second marriage to Francis took precedence and there was no financing to be had. Marsha never supported Katherine's dreams, even when they became more realistic. That ended Katherine's pursuit of dancing, although she always considered herself a dancer. We were like gypsies on opposite ends of the world, destined to come together some day.

Upon graduating high school, Katherine left home to live on her own. She moved from place to place with different men, but always carried a clear sense of her values. She was not materialistic, but spiritual in so many ways. She took college classes here and there and she kept dancing for pleasure, even joining in a small dance company for a brief time. She experimented with drugs, as was common in the '70s and tried taking Ritalin to help her through her long days of classes and supporting herself. Boomeranging in and out of her mother's house and different jobs, her stability was limited. More men came and went for Marsha. Katherine, always the acute observer, learned as best she could from her mother's marital and relationship mistakes. In time, Katherine became good friends with a man named Daron and they moved in together. Within a year Daron had asked her to marry him. Katherine thought long and hard and happily said, "Yes".

A few weeks later, after their engagement, Daron went to Lake Tahoe on business, but did not return as planned. Katherine spoke to his father and then his brother and was feeling anxious at his disappearance. Another week had passed before Daron called to say he had eloped with someone else and had been on his honeymoon. Katherine was baffled and extremely hurt, having no clue about his involvement with someone else. More hurt and lost than ever before, she felt unworthy of love and a real relationship. She fell ill, lost her job, and had no money. Her survival skills were waning. The vagabond life was losing its appeal until Dave came along.

Another handsome, nice man from the valley, Dave came into the restaurant where Katherine was waiting tables and came over to her as she counted her tips. He handed Katherine his business card and asked her to give him a call. To her astonishment, on their first date he appeared in a Rolls Royce. They walked and talked for hours. They danced and kissed and later, he called again and again. Dave was gracious and generous and helped to lift Katherine out of a life that felt like it was going nowhere. He bought her beautiful new clothes and many other comfort gifts that led to her moving in with him and enjoying his social circle. Although Katherine became pregnant, she lost the baby shortly by miscarriage.

Soon Dave's stories became more elusive and as Katherine continued to waitress, Dave became stranger and stranger. His talk about filling government contracts for his father who worked for NASA seemed far-fetched, when there was no apparent warehouse and little office space for Dave's work. He claimed he had an MBA from the Wharton School of Business at the University if Pennsylvania, but she never could quite figure out exactly what he did. When there was an obscure phone call on Dave's answering machine, Katherine became suspicious. Screening the call made her feel untrusting as she tried to piece the puzzle together. Shortly after the overheard message, Dave asked Katherine to go to Europe on a trip with him. He began to tie up loose business ends, pack up the apartment and somehow, they ended up in Arizona, where they lived for a while until they drifted apart. There was a vague story about embezzlement and millions of dollars, counterfeit money and prison. Katherine was lost at knowing what the truth really was. She was glad the relationship had long since soured and that Dave had left her a little place of her own to live in. She was settled in and then she met a handsome young foreign student, Anders, while out dancing in a night club.

Anders was a highly educated Swedish man, attending a small private business college in Arizona. He was funny and silly and spoke seven languages. He was very attracted to Katherine and began courting her. But Anders became disheartened with the school he was attending and returned to Sweden. He called her from Europe and wanted to come back to her and the States. She remembers thinking, "He's fallen for me, I don't know why." So, Anders returned, they got an apartment in Glendale, California and Katherine thought it was "all good." They had friends, went to movies, ate and drank, and truly enjoyed each others company. She was drawn to his "goofy" behavior and his European Monte Pythonesque sense of humor. She wasn't big on the two different colored socks in public that he wore, but she let Anders be who he was and he let her grow and thrive.

Her next attempt at beauty school was a wash, so to speak. Katherine had a major problem touching all those strangers, so when Anders graduated with his MBA and asked Katherine to join him in Sweden for his next position working for a company similar to Club Med, Katherine closed up their little apartment and flew to Ander's mother's apartment in Sweden. Siv was a wonderful woman, always remaining close to Katherine for years to come. She cooked for her and together they would go to the green grocers and buy fresh mushrooms and cheap wine. Anders headed off to the Canary Islands and eventually sought more permanent employment in Spain. Katherine left the cozy environment of Siv's home and joined Anders in the sun and warmth of Madrid. They lived comfortably in a small apartment. Katherine did the marketing and tried to learn Spanish as Anders worked. They lived on flour tortillas, rice, fresh baked bread and beans. It was a quiet and simple, yet content life.

Back in Florida, Katherine's brother Tim was getting married and after a long time with no communication, Katherine got a call from her mother and her brother. They were high after partying from the wedding and Katherine's tolerance was short. She realized that she really didn't know her own family any more, that they were never going to change and that she was indeed starting her new life.

Katherine and Anders spent weekends hanging out in Madrid with friends. They listened to Spanish music and watched Flamenco dancers. They had good times together and Katherine has wonderfully fond memories of her time in Europe. Things went along smoothly until Katherine's health came into question and after many visits to various Spanish doctors; confirmation that Katherine was pregnant was evident. Katherine and Andres were not ready for this. Anders did not want to be a father, but told Katherine he would respect any choices that she made. At five months pregnant and on her own, Katherine sought refuge again with her aunt in California and to place her baby up for adoption in hopes of returning to Madrid and Anders soon.

Chapter Eight

1989

October 21, 1989

Dearest Katherine,

I've been meaning to write for a while, but I was also waiting for a response to my last letter (June or July?) before I wrote again. I got concerned that maybe you never got it (it had a picture in it) or that maybe in the midst of our August 1st move, it got lost. I finally got the time to phone Harvey and he told me that you moved a few months ago, too. So—I don't know if you got my last letter or not and I hope it's OK that he gave me your current address. He also gave me your new phone number, but I opted not to call you in case you didn't want that. Should I keep the number in my file?

Well, everything here is great. I don't really want to repeat myself, but I want to let you know what's been going on, so I hope I don't bore you. We sold our house and moved in August to a real suburban neighborhood. It's really nice! Parks all around to walk to and Bruce started preschool! He is a little boy already. An absolute sweetheart.

The biggest news is that I am 8 ½ months pregnant and due at Thanksgiving. With A LOT of medical screening and probing, I've made it this far with a lot of care. I've been fine, and Bruce is going to have a baby sister. He comes with me to the ultrasounds and listens to the heartbeat. We are all ecstatic to no end.

141

Scott's office moved to Oxnard, so he has been busy commuting and working. He's doing fine and enjoys his new house.

We hope that everything with you is wonderful and look forward to getting our next letter.

We love you—

Andrea, Scott and Bruce

October 21, 1989

Dearest Andrea,

Congratulations on your pregnancy! How wonderful that Bruce will have a little sister to love. Praise God and expect miracles! (This is a big part of my philosophy!) Your life sounds very fulfilling, very" together" to use a term from the 70's. I'm so pleased and thankful that Bruce picked you to raise him and take good care of him. He really picked you two—not me—I asked him when he was still within me what he wanted. I finally got to a very still and calm place to listen and to be guided. And, as a result, love abounds in Bruce's life, and as his birth mother—I asked for him to be blessed with positive, healthy, nurturing parents and WALLA/VOILA, he got it! Sure, sometimes his absence from my life is rough to take and people have some pretty adverse reactions to MY story, however, to keep my perspective, I remind myself of who I am and why I chose to let Bruce have the best for his life. Besides, most people have family or friends or some kind of security for their children (hopefully). This however, was not the case for me. The most important concern then, (When Bruce was 'Seren' to me, anyway) and now, is that Bruce be in a positive, healthy, and happy environment. Thanks to you and Scott and God-he got there.

Thanks for including your new phone number-it helps me to feel secure somehow. My situation is this-in a nutshell...

I'm looking to rent a room here in Carlsbad—I'm going after work to look at one today. To put a long story short, I am leaving a negative, unhealthy co-dependent relationship with Stephen and spreading my gorgeous powerful wings for higher ground, so to speak. I already feel a weight of muck out of my life at having made this long needed decision—Harvey and I have talked about this relationship many times.

I've been working as a preschool teacher, but I'm going to hang that up soon—doesn't pay beans and I need to support myself fully.

I also work in a pretty cool restaurant called "Bullys." Bullys is an established part of north county San Diego and has great Prime Rib, lobster, all that good stuff we're not supposed to eat anymore but do.

And I go to Mira Costa College in Oceanside—this semester it's Child Psychology, and Math and Science for Young children. My goal here is to facilitate "Parent Education" groups so sorely needed in this county.

So, that's the latest scoop from my world-nice sharing with you! Thanks so much for the pictures—they're much appreciated, you know! If I had any of me, I'd send them, but I don't right now. I spoke to Anders a while back—he is still in Madrid, doing the same thing.

Okay love—I'm saying good-bye for now—keep in touch—feel free to call me any time—rain or shine.

Love you all,

Katherine

Bruce successfully completed his "We're Having A Baby" class for expectant siblings in October 1989, at Tarzana Medical Hospital, and was certified as a 'Prepared Big Brother'. We completed our Harris Method of Prepared Childbirth Class. A few weeks later, Blaine was born.

Blaine's birth announcement read,
> To be a child is to know the fun of living
> To have a child is to know the beauty of life
> Bruce Zaron Matis
> Has a new baby sister
> BLAINE ESTY
> Born Tuesday, November 14, 1989
> 5 lbs., 8 oz.

Andrea and Scott Matis

I had missed my Arthritis Foundation Board meeting that day, but made it to the meeting agenda with hearty congratulations.

Blaine was in distress in-utero, with the umbilical chord wrapped around her tiny little neck. Each time I pushed during a contraction, the baby monitor signaled. Dr. Rubinstein placed forceps on her head and pulled her out as fast as he could, while the nurse lay on top of me and pushed on my tummy from the other end. Then without another problem, Blaine sweetly arrived.

While I was pregnant with Blaine, my grandmother and matriarch of the Brodsky family passed away. Due to old superstition, I was not allowed to attend the funeral while pregnant. This occurred at the same time as Scott's parent's 50th anniversary in Las Vegas, which I obviously was allowed to attend. It was so difficult for Scott and me to agree on a name. We were definitely going to name the baby for my MomMom whose English name was Esther. But in 1989, that would have been quite a burden to carry such a big name for such a little baby! So we decided we would use Esther as her Hebrew name and then pick anything we wanted for her English name. This started a huge research campaign, reading movie credits, baby name books, Blue shield doctor lists and various other lists of names. We went from A to Z and still could not agree. Then it popped into my head. A name I had heard while working at Breakdown Services that I thought was the coolest name, especially for a girl. I knew no one else with the name, so as common as I thought the name Bruce would be (there was never another Bruce in preschool, elementary school, high school, anywhere) I knew that there would be only one Blaine. The original Blaine was the wife of my dear friend John at work at Breakdown Services, and as soon as I thought of it, we both agreed to stop searching any further and Blaine would be the baby's first name. John was the man who approved of Scott as my husband. After eight years of dating each other (and some others), I just knew Scott was going to ask me to get married. I just needed an unbiased opinion to confirm if he was the right man for me forever and ever. John and I left the Breakdown offices and headed to El Coyote on Beverly Boulevard to meet Scott for a drink. He actually was in one of the foulest moods I had even seen him in during all the years I knew him. He was having a legal problem with the business next to the Weiner Factory. I felt almost embarrassed to introduce him to John and then later to ask John his feelings which I trusted implicitly. But John adored Scott and gave his approval the next morning at the water cooler. And that was where we got the name, Blaine. We just loved it, so unusual and pretty.

The only other Blaine we have ever crossed paths with was a boy in preschool-we called him boy Blaine. Everywhere we took our smiling beauty, people would ask her name. Unlike Bruce, wherever we took him, people would ask if it was a boy or a girl because he was so stunning. But whenever we told someone Blaine's name, we always got the same response, "What a great name!" Still concerned about her middle name, we decided to make one up. We took Esther, shortened it, and made up Esty. It fit perfect.

January 3, 1990

Dearest Family,

Congratulations to you (us) for the birth of Blaine Esty. Indeed I know the beauty of giving life—indeed....
You all look healthy and happy in the pictures you were kind enough to send me. Thank you very much.
How do you like living in Oxnard? I imagine it's a lot different than living in 'the valley'. It took me a while to receive the announcement and pictures (got 'em yesterday) because I moved again.

Now, long story made short...I separated from Stephen in order to live a happier life, more independent and spiritual life. So far—so good. Of course, it is complicated. I have lived/loved this man/child for over 9-10 years total. Anyway, Stephen is my friend still, but as far as a woman/man relationship...NO! He was important and supportive when I came back from Spain with Seren in my womb. He helped support me emotionally and rationally to keep me steady enough to choose the best life for Seren that I possibly could. And, he helped me afterwards, when my grieving heart weighed so heavily with loss. To give life, out of love and respect for that which is dearest to you—truly costs and yet in contrast is to rejoice in the name and image of God.

Thank God for allowing Seren who was to become Bruce to come through me to be grown by you two-loving souls.

Forgive me for making this short—but it's difficult for me to write sometimes. My best wishes for a long happy healthy life.

Yours always,

Katherine

P.S. Did Bruce have a Happy 3rd Birthday Monday? I'm sure he did!!

April 30, 1990

Hi All!
I'm writing to let you know my new address (no

phone yet) and to let you know I am thinking of you. How are Bruce and Blaine getting along? What's new with you? I'm still working at the same place and looking forward to taking acting and singing classes next semester. Hopefully, I'll be able to do both but, if not, I'll opt for the acting class.

My roommate, Delfina, has had to move back home because she couldn't make it financially at the salon she was at—sooo-I had to find a room (with a view of our lagoon) for myself. It's 3 blocks away from where I've been living. I guess I'll like it-we'll see.

I miss hearing from you—if you get a chance, Andrea, drop me a line or two (pictures are wonderfully received too!). I know you're probably really busy. I love you all!

God Bless Bruce and his family,

Katherine XXOO
P.S. In rereading this letter before sending it off this morning—I sound somewhat superficial—I sound sort of "hunky dorey!" Know me—know me—know me—I have shared my soul with you—words for this do escape me. My talent for expression seems so lacking at this medium called writing.

After a miraculous pregnancy and birth, and sitting on a 'donut', (a circular cushion device for my sore bum) for weeks because I just didn't stretch enough for my delivery like most people with normal tissue and had a very bad delivery tear, life in the Conejo Valley started to proceed. The hospital staff wheeled me to the curb with Blaine in my arms. I was told at the birthing class to make sure to buy something new to wear home from the hospital so I felt special. I wore my brand new Peter Max sweatshirt and black leggings. I loved that top.

Now, it was time to start researching preschools for Bruce and starting Gymboree for Blaine. We finally decided on the Temple school, where we had joined as members. Bruce was very talkative and social and as a mom, I participated in activities and fieldtrips. We hired a Nanny from Indiana only to find out her reason for coming to California was to be near her boyfriend at UCLA and get her residence status so that she could go there the following year. She stayed with us a short time, and after we brought Blaine home from the hospital, she gave us notice. As horrified as we were to lose someone who was so good with Bruce, Scott couldn't wait to get her and her Miss Personality Contest Winner Personality (NOT!) out of his house.

November 26, 1990

Dearest Andrea and Family,

Hello to all of you! I do apologize for not having written sooner! I'm very busy working in three restaurants. All P/T—but business slows down in the winter months in this tourist town and so a girl's gotta do what a girl's gotta do! Needless to say—I have no life right now. I'm kidding. I usually have fun on the job—playing with people.

Did you all have an enjoyable Thanksgiving Day? I had a fun day (no work) reading on the beach and then went to dinner at my friend's house. It was a big family

*with grandmas and grandpas and aunts and uncles,
cousins, moms, dads, children of various ages—the whole
nine yards. Fun!!*

*I'm enclosing some photos for Bruce and you guys,
too. Hope they're not too scary!*

*I'm wishing you all a very Happy Hanukah and
peaceful Holiday Season.*

With all my heart,

Katherine

We placed ads in the local paper and were soon
interviewing a twenty-year-old German au pair who was
not happy at her current employment. We hired Ilka on the
spot and never thought twice about it. She was incredible.
Smart, worked all the hours she said she would and was
simply wonderful with Bruce. She took on the diaper
changing for Blaine that was so difficult for me, the bathing
and even driving Bruce to school some mornings. My life
with two children was smooth and so much less stressful
due to Ilka. We were blessed once again. We loved her.
My parents loved her. My sister loved her. She so wanted
to stay on past her visitors visa, but refused to do so
illegally. So, she planned to go home, revamp and come
back soon. So we waited. But Ilka's own father became
very ill and she could not return as planned. So SHE took
out an ad in her local paper in Germany and sent us a new
au pair. Initially, this girl had problems that were very well
hidden and that slowly surfaced. Although I very much
enjoyed having my tea and toast on the table each morning,
I simply could not raise another child, certainly not one

with a major eating disorder. We found moldy food and knives and other eating utensils hidden underneath her bed and when we tried talking to her, it simply did not go well and she wanted to leave. So we placed another ad in the papers and were soon on the phone to a lovely young lady phoning from Colorado who was looking for a new nanny position in California.

The next thing we knew, we were picking up Rika, originally from Hamburg, Germany, at LAX and bringing this tall, beautiful, sweet woman back to our home. She reminded me of the actress Sean Young when she was in her prime. Like Ilka, she went with me everywhere I needed her. The kids loved her. She bought herself an old light blue Volkswagen beetle from our mailman and a long board, made friends and enjoyed all that SoCal could offer. Rika was with us when we celebrated Blaine's first birthday. Already walking for months, Blaine was an independent child from early on. I would sit her on the floor in the family room at 6 months with a pile of toys in front of her and she would play while I showered, folded laundry and drank my tea. When I went to visit Cindy, Bruce played with her dogs and Blaine would sit on my lap at age seven months, listening to the conversation for forty-five minutes, watching, and not squirming.

One day, Rika wanted to go to a museum. So we packed up Bruce, Blaine, the Cheerios, bottles and diapers and headed to the Norton Simon Museum in Pasadena. You know the one you always see as the floats go by on New Year's Day for the Rose Parade. Not checking the opening time, we arrived somewhat early, but we were allowed to walk around the outdoor sculpture garden until the doors opened. Bruce started to get fidgety as we wandered through the Rodin exhibit and asked when we could go inside. To distract him, I asked him what the big statue of the man was doing (The Thinker). He looked carefully at the giant statue and said to me, "He's thinking". I asked him, "What do you think he's thinking about?" And with all that honesty and truthfulness that comes with being three years old, he looked at me and replied, "He's thinking about going into the museum!" Rika and I busted up. How perceptive kids are! It made me flash back to Bruce's first visit to a museum. He was four months old when we took him to the Museum of Modern Art (MOCA) in New York City. While looking at a Jasper Johns painting of an American flag, an old woman came up to me while I was holding Bruce on my shoulder and said, "That is the most beautiful work of art in this museum." Indeed.

August 21, 1990

Dear Katherine,

I know it's been a while, but it has been a "long, hot summer." I didn't have any help with the kids the month of June; even with my hand surgery it is tough. In July, I had really lousy help. Bruce wouldn't even play with her, and then no help again until August. So—I haven't had a minute to do anything else! At the end of June, we went back to Philadelphia for a family reunion. The pictures are from my cousin's backyard and from a theme park called "Sesame Place" where Bruce climbed Cookie Mountain! He had a blast. Scott's doing real well in his food brokering business and in two weeks, I start teaching again for the Arthritis Foundation. I taught last spring too. I also registered for another painting class today. I haven't painted in a year! Blaine weighs about 19 pounds and is adorable. She's learning to ward off her big bro! We hope all is well with you and look forward to your next letter.

All our love,

The Matises

Blaine's calmness and independence were striking for her age and my mom would say, "She knows she needs to be good and help you!" Sometimes I thought she did. Now, Blaine was turning one year, Bruce was almost four. Scott and I had the life we thought we would NEVER have together five years prior. I put on my black and white hounds tooth leggings with my new black turtleneck tunic and headed down to entertain family and friends for Blaine's first birthday party. "You look great. How are you feeling? Are you managing ok?" were the phrases of the day. Scott and I were so happy. Out of nowhere, I had a thought.

"Wasn't my period due last week?" How strange. I was never late, well, not unless…wait a minute. What is going on here? I got a bit distracted from the party and came back to focus on my guests. After everyone left, I told Scott what I was thinking. Rika overheard and immediately offered to go to the market and buy a home pregnancy test. I had never bought one before-why would I? But back then you had to do the test first thing in the morning, so we waited. We were accustomed to waiting for things all these years. We were actually getting quite good at it.

The next morning, I peed onto a little plastic cube and within seconds a small '+' appeared. Scott and I stared at each other. What is going on here? I got on the phone and called Dr. Rubinstein's office for an appointment.

I headed back to the Valley to visit with my second favorite doctor, Peter Rubinstein. He did a blood test to confirm his physical exam and the next day, I knew I was pregnant. Now, this was truly a miracle. I had been with Scott seventeen years and had NEVER been pregnant on my own! How did this happen? Sex after Blaine's birth was no fun for months and then two kids and two dogs later, time was limited. All in all I would say we had sex maybe a dozen times that year. And of course, all without the diaphragm I received on my six week check up after Blaine's delivery. Why would I ever use that? I was still watching the calendar after all these years and knew there was no way I could get pregnant on Day Ten of my cycle. WRONG! Dr. Rubinstein asked if I had been using my diaphragm and I said, "Why?" "Well, now that you delivered and stretched out your cervix, I believe that is why you couldn't conceive prior to Blaine, and now you have!" Who'd a thunk it!

I zipped my mouth shut and Scott and I went to celebrate with dinner at Wolfgang Puck's restaurant Chenois, on Main Street in Santa Monica. We could not wipe the smiles off our faces. Crispy fried spinach, give me the whole plate. Fried Catfish. I'm eating for two! And I did. And I began to gain weight faster than last time. And everyone thought I looked so healthy at 112 pounds. And happy. And then suspicions ran wild.

We survived not telling anyone through our anniversary at Thanksgiving and early December. But the holidays soon rolled around. I was only eleven weeks along when we went to dinner at Scott's sister's house for Hanukkah, Aunt Michele's. All the Matises were there. I was beaming. I had some meat on my bones. We were all hanging around in the kitchen. Scott and I had agreed not to tell anyone that we were pregnant until I had completed my first trimester, (just a few more weeks away) for good luck (that "Let's not jinx anything" idea again). But Scott's niece, JJ, commented on how healthy and glowing I looked, "Like you looked when you were pregnant last year." She said. My poker face was gone. I couldn't find it anywhere. "Aunt Andrea? Are you pregnant?" I was still searching for my poker face. "Uh, uh, well. We weren't going to say anything, but, yes!"

Scott's parents were in shock. "You're kidding!" said his mother, Millie. "No, it's true." I could see a piercing glare from Scott's sister. Disbelief. She had just adopted her second child, the half sibling to her daughter Emily. We were all so thrilled that her story was so wonderful. The same birth mother came to her when she was pregnant again to say she wanted Michele to raise her baby. True siblings. And yet, each time she told me that adopting and giving birth were exactly the same, I always knew that yes it was and that no, it was totally different as well. I don't believe she ever took the courses we took about adoption having used an attorney and we always felt she may have had issues regarding infertility and adoption different from our own experiences regarding adoption.

And so now it was time to tell my family and soon everyone knew except the little old ladies I taught arthritis exercise programs to because I didn't want them to think I would stop teaching them. And I didn't. But after several months, it was evident. I was just a regular mom with two kids and one on the way. The Jazzercise ladies I exercised with at the dance studio never even had a clue. They were in shock when I walked back into class six weeks later with a baby in a car seat rocker. People everywhere stopped me and touched me and looked at my beautiful children and I would gloat.

And in my heart I knew that I was the luckiest woman in the entire world. I had a husband who has stuck by my side through thick and thin. As Scott has often said, "In sickness and in health. But it's the health that is the easy part." I had two amazing children that I couldn't take my eyes off of, and I had actually conceived on my own for the first time in my life. An adoption, a fertility baby, and a natural conception. Friends would ask, "Do you want a boy or a girl?" Strangers would ask, "What are your other children? Boy? Girl?" And my response would remain the same, "I have one of each," And soon I did have one of each. Sooner than I thought I would.

April 25, 1991

Dear Andrea, Scott, Bruce & Blaine,

 It's been a long time since we've written each other. I trust all is well with you.
 The latest with me is that I am getting married to my dear friend, Mark Kelley. I hope to be wed July 20, 1991. The details still need to be worked out. We're getting married outside in our yard (it's about ½ acre) and it will be a small wedding. The reception following after will be most of Carlsbad! The reason I say "I hope" to be wed on that day is because three nights ago, I had a very

bad fall at work and broke my femur and hip joint. If this letter doesn't make sense in some places, I had to take morphine for the pain and it takes it's toll on my ability to write. I had surgery (pins and plate) last Tuesday (three days ago) and I'm healing very well. The surgery went real well. I'm in Tri-City Hospital in Vista, not far from home. Needless to say, I can't wait to get out of here! Everyone on this floor snores, snorts and screams! I can't get a good night's rest. Naturally, my doctor is not here this weekend. But, I'll be out soon.

I should heal without complications; it will take three months however. Meanwhile, I'll have plenty of time to plan for our wedding.

How are the children? And you two? I will send some pictures and write real soon. I love hearing from you!

All my love to you all,

KATHERINE.

~ Serenaid ~

Chapter Nine

The Room Began to Shake

May 13, 1991

Dear Katherine,

Congratulations on your upcoming marriage. We are SO happy for you. We are also sorry to hear about your fall and hope you are home by now. We have more incredible news to share with you too…I'm pregnant again! Due at your wedding! We are simply amazed—first time in eighteen years I've ever gotten pregnant by Scott with no help from a doctor! A miracle…we're going to have a big wonderful family. Bruce is very excited and keeps kissing my tummy. Blaine won't know what hit her, but she does love babies. We are all so happy. And exhausted. I did a couple of great paintings this year. My sister Miriam is getting married and I may have to part with the one of them. I told her she could have if she ever married Michael she could choose any of my paintings. She has said she wants "The Tango Dancers", Mir and Michael met in a Ballroom dance class.

Bruce is doing great in preschool. Sings (always), spells etc. Such a sweet boy, and so handsome!

Hope to hear from you soon. Take good care. We ALL love you.

Andrea, Scott, Bruce and Blaine

This is Jeopardy!
"We'll take names that begin
with 'B' and end
In 'E' for 1,000 Alex"
And on the inside...
Who is Brooke Ronit Matis?
Bruce and Blaine's new sister!!
Born---June 26, 1991
Height---18 inches
Weight--- 5 lbs., 8 ½ oz.
Andrea and Scott Matis

Brooke was very excited to enter the world and couldn't wait another day (or week or month). Although her due date was July 26th, she arrived over a month early, on June 26th. I began having those same cramps I had had the year before, twelve days before Blaine's due date. I got up and used the bathroom and got back into bed moaning. Scott got up and asked what was wrong. I had been to the doctor just the day before and everything was fine with the fetal monitor, even though several women at Blaine's Gymboree group commented that I looked tired and pale. So, I began timing the awful pains I was experiencing, thinking they could be early contractions. When they became regular, I told Scott. He called Dr. Rubinstein who said, "What are you waiting for? Get her to the hospital." I wanted to wait for Bruce's preschool carpool; once they arrived to pick up Bruce, we left Blaine with the nanny and bolted to Tarzana Medical. Scott had always wanted a police escort and sped as fast as he could onto the Kanan Road entrance of the Ventura Freeway, but as luck would have it, no highway patrol were around that morning. We made it to the hospital in record time.

I had not even gone to the hospital for my pre-admitting paperwork yet and had to sit in the admitting office in writhing pain while we filled in the necessary forms. I kept thinking that I didn't remember it hurting like this with Blaine. By the time I was taken up to a room, the contractions were getting stronger and closer together. I dressed in a hospital gown in between contractions, and immediately my water broke. I redressed before the doctor made it up to my room. He had to pry my legs apart to see how much I was dilated. I didn't want him to touch me! My knees were locked together like super glue. I hadn't remembered it hurting like this when I was in labor with Blaine. With Blaine, I remember at four centimeters I received my first dose of an epidural and the pains subsided almost immediately. But now, I was already dilated to eight centimeters and was heading to the delivery room at any minute. I had gone way further and much quicker in my labor, no wonder I felt so much more pain. I begged for an epidural and by the time the anesthesiologist arrived, I didn't think I could bear one more contraction. I got the epidural just in the nick of time. Within ten minutes, I gave birth to another new baby girl, weighing the same 5 ½ pounds. The doctor told me that was all my body wanted to stretch. That was as big as I would get. Brooke had been is distress in-utero with a short umbilical cord. Every time I pushed to get her out, she was literally choking. The doctor used a suction cup on the top of her head and pulled her out quickly to relieve her distress.

Her early arrival left us without a name we could agree on. When the nurse came to do the birth certificate form, I asked her to come back the next day. My husband and I were not in agreement for a name yet. I nursed my new little baby girl as we went through every name all over again. I went to bed that night knowing that at least we had agreed on the name Brooke and that her middle name would be for my pen-pal from Israel when I was ten, Ronit. I had always loved that name. And when I had met Ronit when I was seventeen in Israel, she was beautiful, fun and a charming young woman.

When I woke up the next morning, the nurse brought Brooke in to my room to be fed. While I was holding my little baby, the room began to shake. The nurse ran back in and said, "Don't look out the window" as she pulled the curtains closed. "The hospital is on rollers, the shaking looks way worse than it really is." I thought, I can't believe I have come this far to die in an earthquake! I was petrified. "Please stay with me" I yelled at the nurse, but she was off to help other patients. And then the room stopped swaying. Another glorious day in Los Angeles. I took a deep breath. All was well. I immediately called Scott to ask if he had felt the quake and to say Happy Birthday. I was to bring his daughter home on his thirty-seventh birthday. She was to share a two crib bedroom in mauve and ecru with her big sister Blaine. Scott did not feel a thing while he was showering at home, but from the tone of my voice, he knew to rush to come and get us right away.

July 8, 1991

Dearest Andrea & Family,

Hi-hope this note finds you all healthy and happy. I am doing well—I'm going to physical therapy three times

162

per week to strengthen my hip. I'm in my fourth month of pregnancy.

Did I tell you? Mark and I are very excited. I was about to give up on the prospect of having a child—I've tried and tried and tried—finally blessed. Always expect miracles.

Enclosed are some pictures from our beautiful wedding. We had so much fun! Did you have your baby? Write soon, okay? My dearest love to Bruce. I think of him often with faith and strong love.

As always,

Katherine

December 5, 1991

Dearest Andrea et al...

I hope you are having a wonderful Holiday Season. Mark and I are very excited about bringing Chelsea into the world. So far, I've been feeling well and keeping active. I am in my 7th month now. Over the hump, as they say. Mark and I are cooking a Christmas dinner for 25 this year...a true test of our courage. A special hug and kiss for Bruce, please. May your family be blessed with the true gifts of this season...friendship, hope and love. As always...deep love to you all.

Katherine XXXOOO

December 21, 1991

Dearest Andrea et al,

Just a few photos for you. I'm feeling well and so far my pregnancy has been smooth sailing. Getting into launching mode soon. I'm hoping Bruce's birth will have left an easier pathway for Chelsea! How is Bruce doing? Is he a good big brother? I still keep in touch with Anders and his mother should Bruce ever want to know about them.

Any tips on infant care? I've never done this before—I'm a bit anxious. All the best to you Andrea and your wonderful family.

Love-

Katherine

February 18, 1992

Dear Katherine,

We know the date is soon and so here is a little gift. Bassinet sheets, nighties, etc. The green sweater set is from Bruce's Bubbie (grandmother-my mom) with her best wishes. We know everything will be just fine and can't wait to get a picture of Chelsea. You can send mail to our home any time, that's why I wanted you to have our home address. Brooke will be 8 months this week.

We wish you all the best and look forward to hearing from you real soon!

Bruce sends his love.

Andrea, Scott and the Killer B's
(The kids' new nickname!)

February 26, 1992

Dearest Andrea et al,

Thank you so much for Chelsea's gifts! And special thanks to your thoughtful Mother.

I've not got announcements made yet...when I do, I'll send you one. Meanwhile, here are a few photos.

Chelsea was born on Feb. 11, 1992 at 7:26 AM (pulled an all nighter in labor-ugh!) She was six lbs. 12 oz. And 20 inches of beautiful baby! She is a night owl so far and sleeps mainly during the day. She took to the breast immediately after birth and hasn't let go yet! She is doing really well. And I feel somehow graced and rewarded.

How are our beautiful children? Is Bruce enjoying school? Any favorite sports? Is he big? Heard about your heavy rains (this was about the time Chelsea was born). Everything alright with you?

I'll be sending an announcement to you all very soon.

All the best to each of you.

Love always,

Katherine XXOO

~ Serenaid ~

Chapter Ten

Chelsea's Birthday

July 7, 1992

Dear Katherine,

It was so good to hear from you and get those wonderful pictures! We've had a crazy year. In February, we got a lovely new nanny from an Island in Micronesia, Yap. My cousin lives there and helped us. She plans to stay until next summer. Scott got some weird virus right after she got here (CMV) and we really had our hands full for a month or so. Then, Scott got "laid off" and got a new job in April. So, things are finally starting to settle down. In June, Scott's folks took 15 of us on a family vacation to Hawaii. Bruce had a blast, as we did. Now, he's in summer camp & I almost cried when I registered him for Kindergarten. I can't believe it. Blaine knows how to swim and Brooke is 'mama-ing" and "dada-ing" a lot. We have a beautiful family and here are some pictures for you!

All our best, all our love!!

Andrea, Scott, Bruce, Blaine and Brooke

The situation of the live-in help changed repeatedly over the years and by October of 1992, I finally found a wonderful woman, through an agency. Brooki was just over one, Blaine was almost three and Bruce was nearing five years old. The house was getting rather crowded, but we loved her so much. Maby was an incredible cook from Guatemala who was also a nurse in her home country, so not only did she take care of my three children, but she took great care of Scott and me. He loved her food and she grew to call him Mr. Scott and me, Mrs. Andie. As in, "Did you take your vitamins Mrs. Andie?" She also referred to my children as "My kids" and so another extended family was forming. She had a twelve year old daughter, who she paid someone else to watch all week long while she lived with us. Maby would visit Glendy on the weekends, yet I could tell she always feared for her safety.

When the winter holidays rolled around, I invited Glendy to stay with us over the winter break from school. We celebrated Hanukkah and Christmas and grew into one big happy family. It pained me that Maby was separated from her daughter and after much thought, Scott and I invited Glendy to come and live in Maby's room permanently. I got Glendy registered into the local middle school where she went from not knowing a single word of English to slowly becoming fluent. Mr. Scott helped her with her math homework and she helped Maby cook and play with the kids. When we took Bruce and Glendy to the Dodgers game that summer, we joked about our two adopted children! Ten years later, when it came time for Glendy to marry, she phoned and asked Mr. Scott to walk her down the aisle. She asked Brooke and Blaine to be flower girls and Bruce to be an usher at her wedding. We all walked her proudly down the flower laden path. She thanked us all for what we had done for her in her wedding speech. And later, when Glendy gave birth, I felt in some way that I had become a first time grandmother. Maby continued to work less and less for me as the kids grew and finally moved out when Brooke was potty trained. But she still works for us part time to this day.

Way back in 1988, I did a painting. I placed Bruce, Scott and I into the setting of the poolside at the Sunset Marquis Hotel in Hollywood. The pink hotel with the swimming pool was the perfect Los Angeles setting for our family portrait. It was the local hang out at the time for Bruce Springsteen and the E Street Band, so it made sense to paint us there. I was so proud when the painting was completed. There we were, the three of us lounging by the pool. But for some reason, I had forgotten to sign the painting. Several years later, after Blaine was born, I added her into the portrait, with her little pigtails. And again, for some unknown reason, I forgot to sign it. After the surprise birth of Brooki, I again added another crawling child into my acrylic masterpiece. This time, I made sure to sign it. The painting was complete! It hangs in my home today. Our family portrait.

Over the years, I survived motherhood. I took Bruce to preschool, where he was known as the "costume kid." He always wore green, depicting his title role as Peter Pan as he assigned other vital parts as Wendy to little Gabby and Hook to Fran, the preschool director. I went to karate, was a soccer mom, watching Bruce stare at the sky while standing on the field, and worked the softball game (our boy had such a sweet swing) snack shack-my least favorite of any volunteer work I have ever done, having all the kids glare at my hands. Bruce moved on to school plays and Scott and I sat with pride and watched "The Princess and the Pea", "Hamlet", "The Wiz" and "Grease". I listened to him sing and watched him dance, something he inherited from both of his moms! I saw him attempt the trumpet and take piano lessons. He attended YMCA summer camp, religious school to prepare him for his Bar Mitzvah and then on a family vacation to London, met up with the guitar. We were staying with my girlfriend Katy from when I lived in London and she had a son a year older than Bruce who played guitar. Scott and I took bets if his love for the guitar would last more than the usual six months for his other activities. We realized very quickly that the guitar was more than a musical instrument; it seemed to be part of his body. He literally never put it down. The first band was 'Caution' and then to 'Scarlet Rose', all the time writing songs and playing music. He was evolving into quite the musician.

The girls went on with their many activities and I made time to observe them all. We went to ballet, gymnastics, dance recitals, piano, Stargazers, Dance Guard at football games, softball, soccer, dance team, tennis, trampoline team and even the Junior Olympics. I maintained a personal sanity and satisfaction by serving on PTA Boards, Site Council, choreographing the elementary and middle school plays, teaching programs for the Arthritis Foundation and even some Hebrew tutoring on the side. I had a full and crazy busy life. And I had three miraculous children and they were one of each!

When all the kids were young, I took Bruce around to auditions for TV shows, commercials and films. He was so cute as a one year old, a friend gave me the name of an agent and she signed him immediately. Over the next few years, Bruce got to be on a TV show called 'Growing Up Together' with Leeza Gibbons. His name was on his dressing room door at the studio and it was all very exciting. After that, he did a national Mattel commercial and we saw him on TV again. We also started his savings account. His sense of humor expressed itself over and over. His drawing of the father and baby octopus at age 7, titled, "The Evolution of Fatherhood," summed it up with the carton quote, "Pull my tentacle".

May 10, 1993
Dearest Andrea et al…

Just a note to let you know the latest BIG NEWS! I'm pregnant! We are expecting a boy in September. I only found out a month ago. Long story…no periods as I was still breastfeeding Chelsea. No A.M. sickness (never get it), NO CLUE! Went for an amniocentesis last week. It will take two weeks to get the results. We are all happy and excited and surprised. We've moved to a larger place. I got Chelsea's birthday card. Thank you so much for remembering. I trust all is well with you all. A belated Happy Mother's Day.
Forever Yours-

Katherine
BBBASBBBAS
XXXXXOOOOO

July 23, 1993

Dear Katherine,

I have been meaning to write to you since I got your last letter with its wonderful news. I'm so excited—just two months away. What names have you got up your sleeve?

I don't remember if I told you about our latest

171

workshop at Vista—but—it was in March for four weeks. On the last night, we ran into your Harvey. He sent his very best to you and it was great seeing him. Ruben Pannor led the class and as before, it was incredibly interesting. Scott and I can't help but feel so special when we think back on all that had happened prior to Bruce's adoption and how blessed we were to have people like you (a person like YOU) come into our lives at that time—we were absolutely convinced that he would be our only child and how thankful we were that my health slowly turned around and that Bruce now has a big family with two sisters. I often wonder if other people's lives have as much meaning to them as ours has to us! We are so happy to have such close contact with you. It is indeed a miraculous situation. Thank you for everything!

I'm sending a few pictures-and yes, that was Bruce's school picture this year—the worst! But the other is cute. He loves school—and is even loving the summer school—a program offered for the enrichment of education. Next week, he starts camp for four weeks. He has his yellow belt in Karate and starts AYSO soccer in first grade. He lost his first tooth on Monday night. Time does fly!

I hope you are feeling good—let us know the news as soon as possible.

All our love,

Andrea, Scott and the Killer B's

September 18, 1993

Dearest Andrea and Family-

He's here!   Torrey Adam Kelley was born September 10, 1993 at 3:31 A.M. He is 20" and weighed 7 lbs. 4 oz. He is healthy and very sweet tempered. Lucky us!!

Chelsea loves her little brother and is eager to help us take care of him.

How is Bruce doing in school? Sounds like he is a busy guy! That's great! And what a handsome fellow! I'll send a picture of Torrey when we get a good one. Until then-

My love to all of you

Katherine

October 10, 1993

Dearest Matis Family,

Thank you so much for the gifts. Chelsea loves her P.J.'s cause she can make the zipper go up and down! The sweater is beautiful too! Bruce looks so happy and healthy! Thank you for everything, Andrea.

Today is Torrey's one month birthday! He is doing really well—he's filled out a lot in this short amount of time. He's breastfeeding like a pro!

Chelsea and Mark just came back from their bike ride and things are beginning to stir—so I'd better get with the program! I really appreciate your package. Thanks again.

I love you all,

Katherine

In 1994, a dear friend of my sister, Miriam, began working with her Sociology professor at UCLA on research for a book about childcare in America. This detailed interview led to my appearance on the Phil Donahue Show. Benita came to the house on Medea Creek Lane several times to interview me about the hiring of child caregivers. She knew that due to my hand disabilities, I had to have help in the home at least while the kids were in diapers. We began to count up how many women had come to work or live with the Matis family, and it numbered twelve! There were many different types of ladies, from housekeepers, to aux pairs and somewhere in between. Their workloads differed for each one as my needs changed. They would watch the kids while I taught exercise programs for eight years for the Arthritis Foundation, they would clean, do laundry, bathe the kids, and whatever the agreements were. Benita thought it amazing how many strangers I let into my home and exactly how I went about my decision making process in the hiring of these women. When her professor at UCLA started writing a book about the many situations working woman and other women confronted nowadays, I became one interview in many.

Early in 1995, I received a phone call from the offices of the Phil Donahue Show in New York City. They wanted to know if I could be a guest on the show. When I asked what the subject would be, they were very vague. I asked several times, but the only information I received was that it was a program on childcare and that a woman named Julia Wrigley, who wrote a book called *Other*

People's Children was also on the show. Benita's professor. The producer from Donahue said that Ms. Fields was so impressed by my interview written with Benita for her book, that she thought I would be an outstanding guest on the topic. After much consideration, I flew by myself that April (they would not pay for my husband to escort me) to NYC and stayed at a hotel near Lincoln Center. I dined with our old college girlfriend, Leslie, who wrote one of my recommendations for Vista Del Mar and awoke bright and early to take my Limo ride to the studio. It was a beautiful New York morning and I was feeling so very important.

I arrived at the taping and was asked to wait in the Greenroom. My makeup was fine and alone I waited for my directions. Soon, another woman entered the room and I introduced myself. Having learned to be more socially outgoing through volunteer work with the Scleroderma Foundations and PTA, I asked why she had been asked to be on the show. This was when I knew I was in big trouble. "My nanny killed my child". On no! This was going to be disastrous. I had no idea what was coming. I kind of went into a fog. I watched the overhead TV with breaking news. A bomb had gone off in the Federal building in Oklahoma City. There was panic everywhere and I felt panic in my chest. My heart was pounding. I was all alone with a woman I didn't know. Then, Julia came in and we met for the first and only time. I was relieved to see her. We talked and I calmed down. But I couldn't focus and was very distracted.

Cynthia, my Oak Park next door neighbor and dear friend, had loaned me her lovely red jacket (some designer label that I wouldn't know) so that I would look awesome on TV, but by the time the taping commenced, I had no idea what I looked like or what I was thinking or saying. I watched the feed from the Greenroom as the other woman were interviewed and I got ready to go onstage as the last guest of the day. With only several minutes left to tape, Donahue interrogated me. I had no idea what I said. I couldn't remember anything that happened once I hit the stage. I was blown away and horrified at what I may have said or done. When the taxi drove me back to the airport, I felt like I had amnesia, that I had been bamboozled. When I got home and everyone asked how it was to be on the show, I said I had NO idea! I didn't know what I had said or how it all came across. All I knew was that I had a picture of me and Phil Donahue to put on my frig! I let Benita know what happened and she felt so bad for me. I was glad it was over. The show aired in September and months later, when a tape arrived from New York, I was glad to see I hadn't made a total idiot out of myself on the Donahue Show. I actually sounded like I knew what I was talking about. I discussed how I interviewed the nannies, what I looked for, what I felt from their first impressions, asking for references, their education background, what languages they spoke, what kind of visa they had, if they had any legal problems, why they wanted the job (certainly when they asked about money right off the bat, I did not hire them) and how we decided who to choose to hire to assist me in child care giving. I said that after hearing all of the other stories presented on the show that day, that I felt lucky to have been disabled and therefore home with my children and the hired help keeping an eye on things. I was lucky to have mostly hired people who were responsible and had common sense. And I was glad to have survived Donahue's dramatics.

~ *Serenaid* ~

August 5, 1995

Dearest Andrea et al,

    Thank you for your letter and pictures of Bruce! He's getting so big! And such a handsome boy! He always looks so happy—this always eases my heart and makes me reassured he is having a wonderful life. This is extremely important to me—which I think you know and have known from the beginning.

    Maui is different! Sometimes it reminds me of the bar scene in Star Wars! There are a lot of different and diverse people on this island. Mark and the children love living here—I'm still undecided about living here long term. It's beautiful, no doubt—however, it's really hot and dry. I love the sunsets and night skies here. Mark is doing well at his chef job at the Grand Wailea. Chelsea is enjoying preschool P/T and Torrey enjoys doing everything Chelsea does! (except using the potty-chair). Torrey will be two years old September 10th.

    I've been managing a restaurant (Chinese) for a few months now—I've (we've) designed my position in order to let me spend more time with the children—they're still too young. And I've missed being with them at night.

    How are you all? What is Bruce doing? Let me know when you have a chance.

    All my love,

    Katherine

August 26, 1998

177

Dear Katherine,

I am so sorry it has taken me forever to write. The summer had just slipped by. The kids were in three different camps, two different summer schools, the beach, movies, etc. Tomorrow we register Bruce for Middle School and get his class schedule. I wanted to tell you that since he was automatically enrolled, I didn't have to show his birth certificate. I therefore (because Scott and I have been talking about this for a long time) filled in all his paperwork as "Bruce Seren Matis"! You have to get a lawyer etc. to do it all officially and eventually we will, but in the meantime, it's what we are writing on all his forms!

He's a little nervous about Middle School, but I'm sure he'll be just fine. He started playing chess and may join the chess club. I've been busy being a PTA Mom, on the Executive Board and all—first time. The girls are ready to head back to dance and gymnastics and I look forward to school starting next week. Maybe then, I'll get my house in order.

The picture of Bruce in the King Claudius gown is from his production of "Hamlet" with the Oak Hills Elementary School Shakespeare Company. He was AWESOME! <u>WOW!</u>

I hope you and your family are all doing great. You are always in our hearts. Did you see "The Baby Dance" on TV?

Please keep in touch sooner than I did!

Love,

Andrea, Scott and the Killer B's

At the risk of extending my openness, Scott and I decided to send Katherine a copy of Bruce's Bar Mitzvah invitation, after the ceremony occurred. Although I wasn't sure if it was the right thing to do, we felt like she was family and would want it for her Seren files. We sent it to her after the event with the personal clarification that we wanted her to have it, but not to have felt obligated to come to the actual service or to have sent a gift. It was a magnificent day. The service was perfect and the celebration afterwards at Duke's on the beach in Malibu was lovely. I wore my teal silk dress the second most expensive outfit I ever owned next to my wedding gown to match Scott's and Bruce's ties and the girls wore casually dressy dresses to match as well. The pictures looked beautiful. Katherine's response to this act of kindness we shared with her was overwhelming.

January 29, 2000

My Dearest Andrea,

I received Bruce's Bar Mitzvah package. I love you for sending this to me. This touches me in ways unimaginable to us all. It's all good.

I was brought back to a reality in life and possibly a tragedy wherein God prevailed and listened to us. When Seren was within my body, I asked him to guide me to the choices of his life. We spent many silent nights, afternoons, whatever time we had to be still enough to listen to ourselves and to our God, in order to know this destiny of

Seren's.

The Powers that truly be—sat and listened—heard the heartfelt wants and pleas and put forth into positive motion. Meanwhile, we mortals waited for this <u>special</u> child to come to us and <u>choose his life</u>. Seren spoke with certainty---it was you he chose. You're his answer to life. I will always love you and Scott for giving Bruce/Seren all your love. Thank you!

God Bless and Keep You,

Katherine

January 15, 2001

Dear Katherine,

It is truly amazing that after all these years we can still be in such close contact and continue our relationship on so many wonderful levels. I want you to know that I did not mean to shock you by having my mother call from her time share in Maui. I thought about it the last few times she has gone, but didn't know if it was appropriate for you or her. This time, when I found out they were going it didn't even cross my mind NOT to ask her to phone you or even to see you while she was there, especially since my sister would be with her.

I know it took you off guard, but I also knew you would welcome her with open arms and an open heart. First, your call about her calling... I hope I didn't sound distant, as we had company and we were on our way to my best friend Kerry's birthday party (she and her sister wrote me a personal reference 16 years ago for the adoption application!) and I truly wanted to talk to you more, but had to really get going.

I am so happy that you are all well and loving Maui, who wouldn't??!! Anyway (second), I called my dad for his birthday yesterday and since he was with Miriam's husband Michael, watching Tiger Woods, I got to talk briefly to my sis and mom who said they had a lovely time with you and your kids! She said she'd fill me in more on everything when she got back to LA. But she did say <u>one</u> thing that hit the spot and so I am writing to you to discuss this new (yet very old idea to me) matter…She said you said I should write a book…I always have thought about this, but the situation would have to be that YOU would write it with me! Between all of our correspondences over the years, our backgrounds, all the paperwork etc…. I am writing to ask you if you would participate in this amazing project with me.

Before I continue to even contemplate this I will wait to hear from you about how you really feel about all this. I would NEVER do it unless YOU did it with me and we could use letters and notes from the past chronologically to make it the "real thing." I am truly willing to commit to this and take the time to make it a great story… it already is!

I hope you had a good time with my family, I can't wait till the day it is WE who meet again!

XOXOXOX

Andrea

P.S. Before you called on Mother's Day, but we had been in touch about Bruce's Bar Mitzvah etc., I saw an Oprah show that inspired me to write the enclosed letter...then, you called me the same day that his Passport came with his name change on it and last time you called was the day his amended birth certificate arrived. I just feel that there is more than US going on here...as always!

February 12, 2001

Dear Katherine,

Hey, that's a good name for a book! I have found a ton of letters from you. I'm sure mine do not add up in any way to the wonderfulness of them! But, if you found mine, and think they are worth putting together with yours and other ideas (adoption application, pictures, background information on us etc.) then let's move on. I have a call into a dear friend who writes theatre reviews for the LA Times, but will call again to meet with her and see how to get started putting this all together into something interesting and worth reading.

I have only discussed it with my mom and my sis, but am ready to get going. I found the Swedish Midsummer Tree and lots of wonderful cards from you. The earliest dated letter was in April '87, do you think it is the first? It sounds like it may be, but there are so many good ones following...and is all this OK with YOUR family?

Let me know where you are with gathering up materials and if you feel that what you found is printable.

There were also letters from Harvey that accompanied yours that I may like to include, so I will track him down for permission. Keep me posted.

Love,

Andie

March 26, 2001

Dear Katherine,

Today is Sunday and I've turned 47 this week and tried to smile as much as I could! I've been thinking about you a lot. Now, my girlfriend who works for the LA Times is reading our letters and thinking of ideas to get the story out. She is a wonderful person and I will be speaking to her this week. Do you have letters from after 1993? I have organized, photocopied etc. and am meeting with other writers for ideas as well. I know one day it will all start to come together as an incredible project.

Is there anything else you want me to do as of now? What is your exact email?? I can keep in touch regularly that way if possible.

I am off to both girls' softball games in a row while Bruce and his friend Oliver from England play electric guitars in the garage!

Love to all. I'll work on recent pix next time!

Xoxoxoxoxo

Andie, Scott Bruce Blaine and Brooki

Early in the fall of 2001, Katherine called us to say she was finally coming to the Mainland for a Kelley family reunion. We talked and talked and decided that this would be the right time for her and Bruce to meet for the 'Mother and Child Reunion'.

Chapter Eleven

The First Meeting

During the many adoption workshops we attended at Vista Del Mar, it was often discussed when the appropriate time was to have your child meet his birth-mother. The main point being, that no matter how smart a parent thinks his/her child is, that a child does not truly understand adoption until he is old enough to understand sex and reproduction. Then they'll be able to comprehend what took place all those years ago. They suggest that a proper reunion should occur when the child is of college age, mature and ready to deal with feelings that may arise undertaking such a reunion.

In the fall of 2001, Bruce was turning fifteen. He had been playing guitar for a year and had heard about his birth mother since he could remember. I approached him with the topic of Katherine coming to California in December. His middle name had been officially changed to Seren for a number of obvious reasons. Seren was on his High School transcript and his diploma from Middle School and it suited him just fine. He was curious to meet her, but of course was nervous just the same. After a long discussion, he agreed.

On December 12th, I drove to the Moorpark Train Station and waited for Katherine's train to arrive from San Diego. It had been almost fifteen years since we had met at Serenia Park in Woodland Hills and said our goodbyes. The train pulled into the station and I immediately recognized the tall slim woman I had met years before. She had short blonde hair, sparkling blue eyes and a small satchel. We hugged for so long, we could not let go of each other. And then we started talking and it was nonstop from that moment until we got to the Westlake Inn where I reserved Katherine a room for the evening. I watched her as she talked to the woman behind the counter. How friendly she was. Not shy at all like Bruce was. We went to her comfortable room, number 106, and left her things there. It was time for me to pick up the girls from school. They knew she was coming and could not wait to meet this mythical woman. Brooke took to her like it was her own birth mother, so excited to meet her and talk to her about her day. Blaine, the quieter daughter, observed.

We arrived at the house on Medea Creek and by that time I assumed Bruce had walked home from school and was waiting for us. The energy in the house was fierce and there is no way I can describe what came next. I'll let Bruce's own words describe the first meeting. Bruce had been given an assignment in Mrs. Kimbal's ninth grade English class. The assignment was to write an autobiographical incident. He did not show me this paper until weeks after he had written it and received his 'A' grade. It more than described the actual reunion and his feelings of that day as well. Mrs. Kimbal even called me to tell me what a wonderful paper he had written and that she had Bruce share it with the class. He was happy to do so.

My whole body shook with anticipation. I was finally going to meet her. I wondered for nearly my whole life what she looked like, what kind of person she is, whether or not she is mean. So many questions ran through my head as I approached the door. I set down my backpack, sat on my comfortable leather couch, grasping the armrest so I might relieve some stress. It didn't work.

It was then that I realized that I should probably look a little nicer so I could make a good first impression. I knew that on December 12 at 3:15 PM, I was going to meet my birth mother, Katherine Kelley, for the first time.

The moment was soon arriving. I was so scared that I ran upstairs and hid under the bed until my mom would call me down for the first encounter. The sound of the door opening brought a chill to my spine. All the anxiety seemed to rush out of me coming down my arms and out my fingers. I closed my eyes and reflected on all the years I spent wondering about her, and the day had finally come. I heard the voice of my adoptive mother, Andrea Matis. I knew what she was going to say before she said it, and then she did.

"Bruce, Katherine's here," she said as politely as possible. I guessed that she was trying to make a good impression too. The moment was coming. With another deep breath, I slowly opened the door. Without peering out, I took my first step out of the room, trying to act casual though my feet felt cemented to the floor. I walked slowly, hoping not to fall down in front of my birth mother. So many things were rushing through my head. I remembered so many memories from my childhood: the birthday letters my birth mother sent me, all the questions I asked about adoption. It all led up to this point.

I reached the bottom of the stairs, and tilted my head up. My eyes were shut, but there was some tugging force that made me open them. The mixed emotions overcame me, and as I looked at the woman who had given me life, I could only wait for her to make the first move. It seemed like I was standing there for an eternity, just staring in the eyes of my birth mother. She just stared back; it seemed like the whole world around me stopped as she finally opened her mouth. It was then that I felt a strange sense of warmth, and I eased up a bit. She made the first move, and all she had to say was, "Don't worry, I'm nervous too." The same force that made me open my eyes was now pushing me towards her, and as I hugged her for the first time, all I could think of saying was, "Thank you…for everything."

And so, it was done. Katherine told Bruce she was just as nervous as he was but that she wanted a hug. They apprehensively hugged. Quickly, they moved into the kitchen for snacks and the chatting began. Her warmth and inquisitiveness led him to talk about his day at school, his interests and to lead her into his bedroom, where she and I plopped down on his bed and listened while he played his guitar for her. She was both amused and amazed. She adored his music. Scott came home, dinner progressed with Hanukkah gifts for all including Katherine, a hand made garnet and silver bracelet by my girlfriend and soon they were to say their goodbyes. They would meet again the following summer when we planned a family vacation to Maui, Hawaii.

Epilogue

In August of 2002, Scott and I took the three children to Maui to stay at my parents' time share in Wailea. It was two miles from the home of Katherine and Mark Kelley and their two children Chelsea and Torrey. Katherine and Chelsea came by the evening we arrived to say hello. Bruce was now meeting one of his half biological siblings. We knew it was intense for him, but he was sweet and kind. Katherine invited us to dinner at the house Friday evening. Her husband, Mark, and some of his buddies from work were barbequing and jamming on guitars and wanted Bruce to play with them. The vacation was falling into place. We figured we'd see the Kelley's a couple of times, but had no idea we would see them every day for eight days.

Sunsets at the beach, dining out and hiking through the Iao Valley. But what was so amazing was the relationship that also grew between Bruce and Katherine's husband, Mark. Mark accepted Bruce with open arms. That Friday night in August, we sat around and listened to my young teenage son play guitar with three men he had never met. Katherine and I sipped our wine and Scott sat beaming from the floor across the room. One of the guys said, "Dude, what was your name again? Your last name too? 'Cause when you're a famous guitarist, I want to tell everyone that I jammed with you once upon a time."

"Bruce Seren Matis," Bruce replied.

Katherine looked at me with contentment and said, *"Look what we made!"*

~ Serenaid ~

~ Serenaid ~

~ Serenaid ~

A portion of the proceeds from this book will be donated to the Scleroderma Research Foundation. If you would like to contribute to the continuing efforts in improving the treatment, and helping find a cure for Scleroderma, call toll free at, (800) 441-CURE and make a further donation.

You can also learn more about Scleroderma by visiting the Scleroderma Research Foundation's website at:

http://www.srfcure.org

*   *   *

To contact the author, email Andrea Berman Matis at:

andreamatis@sbcglobal.net

*   *   *

Be sure to take a look at all the fine books from Williams Publishing. You may visit our website at:

www.wmpbooks.com

To order more copies of this book or any of our books Contact us via our website or call: (760) 902-1972

Williams Publishing
6176 Driver Road
Palm Springs, California 92264